7.28.94

Gail

Best of luck in your
new position!

Elly Musleh

What The Experts Are Saying About
Feed Your Eagles

"Each reader will take away from Derek Newton's latest book many valuable ideas. For me, his chapter on listening and reflective listening is, alone, worth the price of admission. Very important advice.**"**

> Fred Danzig, Editor
> *Advertising Age*

"Dr. Newton challenges each manager in a way that is so easily understood. His business knowledge and his great case examples only reinforced the message sent in each chapter, and nothing surpasses Newton's Laws for bringing a message home.**"**

> Michael E. Belk, Vice President, Sales
> *Springs Industries, Inc.*

"Derek Newton's common-sense wisdom stimulates excellence in any sales organization. His insight provides a great approach not only to sales management, but to life.**"**

> W. Marston Becker, President
> *McDonough Caperton Insurance Group*

Inspiring and
Coaching Your
Sales Team to
the Top

Feed
Your
Eagles

DEREK A. NEWTON
**The John Tyler Professor of
Business Administration
Darden Graduate School of Business Administration
University of Virginia**

**PROBUS PUBLISHING COMPANY
Chicago, Illinois
Cambridge, England**

ISBN 1-55738-531-9

Printed in the United States of America

BB

1 2 3 4 5 6 7 8 9 0

TAQ/BJS

To: Charlie, again.
And Lindsay, too.

Table of Contents

Preface   vii

Acknowledgments   ix

Introduction   xi

PART I
THE FOUNDATION: LEADERSHIP AND STRATEGY   1

Chapter 1   Overview   3

Chapter 2   Leadership   7

Chapter 3   Strategic Decisions   17

Chapter 4   Marketing Strategy   21

Chapter 5   Desired Sales-Force Behavior   47

Chapter 6   Tactical Decisions   53

Chapter 7   Commitment   59

PART II
THE SYSTEM: POLICIES AND PROCEDURES   63

Chapter 8   Policies   65

Chapter 9   Organization   73

Chapter 10   Selection   83

Chapter 11   Training   91

Chapter 12   Compensation   95

Chapter 13   Incentives   105

Chapter 14   Performance Appraisal   113

Chapter 15   The Invisible Supervisor   123

PART III
THE MANAGERS: CLIMATE AND STYLE   125

Chapter 16   Field Supervision   127

Chapter 17   Climate   135

Chapter 18   Style   143

Chapter 19   Relationships   149

Chapter 20   Activities   163

Chapter 21   Motivation   177

Chapter 22   Managerial Growth   195

PART IV
THE PEOPLE: EAGLES AND OTHERS   201

Chapter 23   Theories   203

Chapter 24   Problems   221

Chapter 25   Opportunities   227

Chapter 26   High Performance   243

Conclusion   253

Index   257

Preface

This book is written primarily for the sales executive and those who aspire to become one. Secondary audiences are those interested in the role of the sales force in implementing business unit strategy and those interested in building and managing a high-performance organization, sales or otherwise.

A high-performance sales organization is the product of strategic thinking, sound policies, tactical action, thoughtful marketing, inspired leadership, great field supervision, interpersonal skill, and basic attitudes regarding personal dignity and respect. I have attempted to address all these areas in this book.

Many of the ideas expressed herein are "unconventional wisdom" derived from my observations of and discussions with hundreds of sales executives from high-performance sales organizations. Part of the reason why these organizations perform so well is that their executives are not afraid to be unconventional—to do things better often requires that we do things differently. One generations's heresy is the next generation's standard operating procedure. Progress is the consequence of creative leadership.

Derek A. Newton

Acknowledgments

Thousands of people have contributed to this book. Some of them I know personally, some I have observed, and some I have only read about. Some of these contributions were made knowingly, and some unknowingly. Nevertheless, whether these people were my students—executive or MBA—my teachers, my friends, or prestigious scholars or anonymous subjects of my observations, I owe all of them a debt of gratitude.

Many people deserve special recognition for their contributions to my growth and development and to this book. At the risk of omitting someone important, let me give the following thanks.

Larry Ring of the College of William and Mary, and Pete Borden and Paul Farris of the Darden School are coauthors with me of a graduate-level marketing text. Their contributions to the marketing side of this book are substantial. My colleagues at the Darden School who teach Organizational Behavior have provided me with a great deal of help. Alex Horniman, in particular, helped me shape many of the ideas in this book.

I have tried hard to acknowledge the authors or inspirers of the ideas in this book wherever possible. The reading list in the section about Managerial Growth mentions some of them. The notions of "I am capable" and "I am lovable" are derived from Sigmund Freud's theories that explore the extent to which work and love are major themes in a person's life.

Tony Athos and I were fellow doctoral students and faculty members at the Harvard Business School during the 1960s. His personal influence on me endures today. The book he coauthored with Jack Gabarro, included in the reading list mentioned earlier, has influenced the objectives and content of this book enormously.

I owe much to a cluster of researchers, many of whom are my former teachers and colleagues at the Harvard Business School. Although I may have bent and tortured their notions of climate and style beyond their recognition, I am particularly indebted to George Litwin, Jay Lorsch, and Robert Stringer, and to the great godfather of organizational behavior, Fritz Roethlisberger. Similarly, I have drawn heavily on the scholarship of Ken Andrews, Chris Christensen, and Bill Guth for the strategy content of this book.

Without the help of Bette Collins and other members of the Darden School editorial staff, this book would be unreadable. In addition, Bette Collins has contributed most generously to the ideas and organization of the material on leadership. Production of the typescript was in the able hands of my competent assistant, Annelise Tew. John Willig and the capable folks at Probus gave me lots of help and valuable advice. The time and money it took to see this project through was provided by the Darden Graduate Business School Foundation under the leadership of Dean John Rosenblum.

Finally, my wife's involvement in this book went far beyond the usual "support and encouragement." She read every word of the many drafts and served as my best friend and harshest critic. It is to her this book is dedicated.

Introduction

I have been privileged to observe and work with a number of high-performance sales forces. The executives in these sales forces are experts in managing motivation. Four key success factors emerge as a common thread in their efforts to manage motivation.

1. Clarity of mission. People from the CEO to the sales reps know what they are doing, understand why they are doing it, and share the same enthusiasm for doing it well. Clarity of mission is the subject of Part I of this book.

2. Sound policies and procedures. The rules and regulations that govern the management of the sales force encourage sales reps to carry out their roles in implementing business-unit strategy willingly and cheerfully, and in line with their personal goals for growth and development. Policies and procedures are the subject of Part II of this book.

3. Commitment to field supervision. Time and resources are devoted to high-quality on-the-job coaching, a prerequisite for high-performance personal selling efforts. Sales-management behaviors are the subject of Part III of this book.

4. Hiring Eagles. High-performance sales-force executives avoid the trap of merely filling territories, because they know it leads in the long term to sales force mediocrity. They concentrate on hiring Eagles.

Although Eagles are the subject of Part IV of this book, the concept of an Eagle is a recurring theme that requires elaboration. Most sales forces contain people who bring in a disproportionate share of the business, who consistently demonstrate high ethical principles and professional behavior, and who are fun to be around. These people are your Eagles. They fly high. They fly free. They are usually easy to spot.

Eagles are authentic people. They are energetic, creative, and make everyone around them feel good. They convert effort into results.

Eagles come in a variety of shapes, sizes, ages, and colors. Some are female; some are male. But they all have one thing in common: They need to be fed.

Eagles thrive on a diet of challenge and recognition. They can't stand being caged, and if ignored, they have a tendency to fly away. Because they produce most of your business, they deserve most of your managers' attention. Because they tend to be eager to learn and quick to master, the payback on your managers' investment in working with them is much higher than a similar investment in developing average or marginal performers. The more a manager shows his or her Eagles that they care about them and that their work is appreciated, the less likely the Eagles are to fly away. To manage motivation, FEED YOUR EAGLES!

PART I

THE FOUNDATION:
LEADERSHIP AND STRATEGY

Chapter One

Overview

Managing motivation begins with business-unit and marketing strategy and continues throughout the organization. The ability to conceptualize at the highest level and translate this conceptualization into an action program at the lowest level is the critical skill of any executive—sales, manufacturing, or financial. Furthermore, the complexities of sales-force management problems require you to understand the consequences of your decisions on all organizational layers. To diagram these relationships, and to provide you with a conceptual framework for building and managing a high-performance sales-force, Figure 1 uses a baseball diamond as a model.

Home plate is the alpha and omega of baseball. The behavior of the customer is the alpha and omega of business. For the ballplayer, no runs are scored unless all four bases are touched. For the marketer, no sale is made until all four bases are touched.

Beginning with an analysis of customer behavior, the marketing executive attempts to match available resources to the risks, opportunities, and constraints in the competitive environment. This matching process results in a marketing strategy—a decision to create customers in a way unique to that business unit. Your sales

FIGURE 1

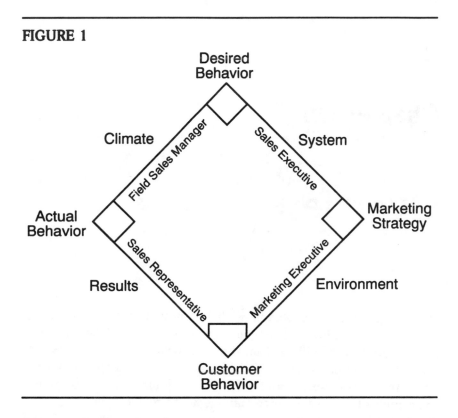

force won't get to first base unless your marketing executives have developed a sound marketing strategy.

Working within the marketing strategy developed for the business unit, the sales executive defines the role to be played by the sales force and creates a management system to support that role. The role is the desired behavior (what you would do if you were the sole sales rep); the system is the combination of policies and procedures selected to encourage the sales reps to behave in a particular manner (as you would behave if you were the sole sales rep). Your sales force won't get to second base unless you have clearly defined the desired sales-force behavior and have chosen that combination of policies and procedures (selection, training, compensation, and so forth) that best encourages that behavior.

Working from an understanding of the desired sales-force behavior, your field sales managers create that supervisory climate that best encourages conformity between actual behavior (what the sales rep does) and desired behavior (what you want the sales rep to do). Your sales force won't get to third base unless your field sales managers ensure that the actual behavior of the sales force conforms to the desired behavior.

In baseball, only runs count, and the only way to score runs is to cross home plate. Similarly, the old cliche in business is, "Nothing happens until the sale is made." Your sales force will cross home plate as often as the actual behavior of the sales rep produces the desired customer behavior.

Clearly, the most effective organizations touch all the bases. To achieve this goal, many people must perform their jobs well. The sales rep must be good at persuading the customer to buy. The field sales manager must be good at teaching and encouraging the sales reps to perform well. You, the sales executive, must be good at defining the role of the sales force on the basis of your business unit's strategy and at creating a set of management policies and procedures to encourage fulfillment of that role. The marketing executive must create an effective overall strategy within which the sales force can operate. Managing motivation begins at the strategic level.

If sales executives don't know where the business unit is supposed to be going or how it is supposed to get there, if they don't know what the business unit is supposed to be doing or how it is supposed to do it, the rest of the sales organization can't be blamed for running around in circles. When target markets are poorly defined, competitive realities are ignored, product lines are ill conceived, distribution channels are hostile, prices are out of line, and advertising messages are confusing, the best sales force in the world is going to have trouble giving the stuff away. Managing motivation—getting your sales force to do what your business unit strategy requires it to do, cheerfully, enthusiastically, and effectively—involves gaining commitment: that sense of doing what's best for everyone.

In analyzing any sales force problem, you should keep in mind the following questions:

1. What is the overall marketing strategy for the product?

2. What is the role of personal selling within that strategy?

3. What policies and procedures have been developed to encourage high performance in personal selling activities?

4. How well are these policies and procedures being implemented?

5. What are their effects on sales-force behavior?

6. What is the role of leadership in making all these things happen?

Chapter 2

Leadership

High performance requires creative leadership. The term *leadership* can be applied to such diverse accomplishments as initiating a new movement in thought, commanding a platoon, or setting a new dress style. Almost as many definitions and methods of approaching the subject exist as there are writers willing and eager to write books about it.

What constitutes and characterizes effective leadership are issues that have fascinated people throughout the ages. These questions are particularly important to people responsible for managing a sales force. Leadership is the management of motivation.

TRAITS

Some people believe that leaders possess certain common personal traits that enable them to become leaders in any and all kinds of situations. A typical list of such traits might include courage, determination, mental adaptiveness, knowledge, and integrity. Some people add skills and techniques to their list—such as the abilities

7

to gain cooperation, to communicate, or to stimulate other people's ideas—in order to make leadership qualities seem less inherent and more learnable.

Not surprisingly, efforts to confirm experimentally any such list of universal qualities have been unsuccessful. Even if it were possible to confirm them, the traits discovered would probably defy precise and practical definition. Some consensus exists, however, that leaders appear to exhibit high levels of intelligence, physical energy, and the desire to lead. These qualities are certainly desirable ones for sales managers to exhibit.

Some writers speculate that successful leaders develop a personal mystique derived from their habits and activities that helps them to achieve their objectives. In the words of the British writer Sir John Hacketts, "If you reach the rank of general without any personal oddities or idiosyncrasies, you'd better go out and get some damned quick."

The concept of leadership as a mystique was introduced by Max Weber, the German sociologist, who used the term *charisma* (the gift of grace) to refer to some extraordinary personal quality, regardless of whether this quality is actual, alleged, or presumed. Charismatic leaders are obeyed by virtue of personal trust in them and their revelations, their heroism, or their exemplary qualities—real or imputed.

In most organizations today, people are limited in their ability to exercise charismatic leadership. Although some executives, such as Lee Iacocca and Ross Perot, appear to appreciate the power of charisma to influence the social scene, most executives, as far as the world outside their organizations is concerned, prefer a low profile to the risk of a bad press.

Nevertheless, many writers stress the desirability of charismatic leadership *within* the organization, the function of maintaining visibility so as to inspire the organization by serving as a focus for emulation. The ability to inspire people is another desirable attribute for sales executives and managers to exhibit. Charisma by itself, however, is insufficient. Indeed, if genuinely qualified people cannot achieve and maintain positions of leadership because they lack charisma, perhaps organizations are doomed to possess leaders devoid of anything but charisma—the image of leadership without its substance. To quote Francis Russell in his biography of Warren G. Harding, *The Shadow of Blooming Grove* (McGraw-Hill, 1968), "But now as the White House gates swung open, the new leader emerged, confident, handsome, virile, and no less the symbolic leader because it was contrary to his nature to lead."

SITUATIONS

One reason that the search for universal leadership traits proved fruitless is that leaders don't function in isolation. They deal with followers within definite cultural, social, and physical contexts. As a consequence, the early emphasis on studying leadership traits shifted toward studying leaders in the context of specific situations. These writers attempted to relate the personal qualities and skills of the leader to the demands of the organization's tasks.

For example, Anthony Jay, the author of *Corporation Man* (Random House, 1971), discussed the phenomenon of multiple leadership within a single tribe, depending on the situation the tribe faces at the time. The necessity to get food produced hunting leaders chosen for their skill in organizing others to pursue the quarry; the necessity to defend the tribe against its enemies produced war chiefs chosen for their courage and strength; the necessity for ensuring tribal continuity produced overall chiefs chosen (or acknowledged) for their wisdom—and perhaps charisma?

Of particular interest is the idea that the relative importance of specific leadership traits varies at different stages of an organization's development. For example, technical creativity and "dynamic salesmanship" may be the critical elements in guiding an organization through its startup stage; organizational and communications skills may be the critical elements during the stage of rapid growth;

and vision and the ability to develop a strong sense of cohesiveness may be the critical elements in maintaining the viability of the mature organization. This view is summarized by the distinguished British author, C. P. Snow, who maintained that great leaders emerge from circumstances and normally do not create them.

Discontinuing the search for leadership traits has never gained total acceptance, however. Leadership traits are still a subject of much research and discussion. Indeed, most of us would probably agree with E. E. Jennings, author of *An Anatomy of Leadership* (Harper and Brothers, 1960), who said, "Great changes in the history of an organization or society generally result from the innovative efforts of a few superior individuals."

RELATIONSHIPS

In the development of leadership theories, the combining of the trait and situation theories to focus on the leadership task led to an examination of the people performing that task and, thus, to an examination of the relationships between leaders and their followers. Theories about the importance of relationships in leadership began to appear in the 1930s and are still influential today. "Relationship" theories were a reaction against the "scientific management" ideas propounded earlier by Taylor, Gilbreth, and others, which were seen as dehumanizing people—treating them as mere resources to be used, ordered, and manipulated by managers. In contrast, relationship theories are based on the assumption that people are more efficient and productive when their needs are understood and satisfied. Work groups that are organized in ways that enable people to help determine their own goals, for example, typically have higher morale and more organizational commitment than those directed by authoritarian leaders. These views, highly relevant to managing motivation in a high-performance sales force, are discussed throughout this book.

Much of the supporting research for relationship theories was conducted by studying small groups in face-to-face situations. These studies spawned hundreds of articles that suggested principles or techniques to be mastered and used to harness human resources. As a consequence, relationship theorists tended to think of leadership more as execution than innovation, more as task accomplishment than task definition. The analysis of leadership in group situations provided managers with new insights and skills in achieving group acceptance of decisions, in conducting group problem-solving activities, in locating the real problems of group concern, and in the emotional and intellectual aspects of group activity. But in the strict relationship approach, group action and the interaction among group members are seen as more important to high-performance outcomes than is the influence of the leader on the group. The leader's function is considered limited to facilitating group processes.

REVISIONISTS

Although relationship theories that acknowledge the importance of human-relations skills to leadership are still popular, they are losing ground to broader definitions of leadership itself. Whereas the relationship theorists criticized scientific management as "organizations without people," a later group of theorists, writing in the 1950s and 1960s, labeled relationship theories as describing "people without organizations" and, in extreme cases, criticized relationship theories for minimizing the role and worth of individuals in relation to the role and worth of the groups to which they belonged. This later group of theorists, called "revisionists," includes such influential thinkers as Chris Argyris.

Argyris concentrated on the relationship between the individual and the organization. His main thesis is that the individual's needs and the formal organization's demands are basically incompatible, because task specialization, chain of command, unity of direction, and so on, make it impossible for the individual to reach self-actualization. In his book, *Personality and Organization* (Harper and Brothers, 1957), he states that the leader's primary responsibility is to "debureaucratize" the formal organization so that the structure provides "increasingly meaningful challenges and opportunity for responsibility." Thereafter, the leader's responsibility is to maintain conditions in which people can behave authentically and openly confront interpersonal differences. Argyris's ideas are important to sales executives and managers as they aspire to create a climate for high performance.

FUNCTIONS

The revisionists sparked interest in studying leadership in large organizations, rather than its application in small groups. The noted psychoanalyst, Jules Masserman, observed that the leader in organizational settings must fulfill three functions: provide for the well-being of those being led, provide a social organization in which people feel relatively secure, and provide people with a single set of beliefs. In this view, the primary function of leadership—that of the chief executive officer, as it were—is the perpetuation of the organization.

The interest in leadership as a function of the "chief executive officer" was brought into particularly sharp focus by Kenneth Andrews. In his *Concepts of Corporate Strategy* (Dow Jones-Irwin, 1971), Andrews talks about the multiple functions of chief executives. As chief architects of strategy, chief executives must have the ability to analyze the strengths and weaknesses of the organization; they must be skilled in analyzing opportunities and risks in the external environment; and in light of their own personal values and aspirations, and with a sense of responsibility to stakeholders and to society as a whole, they must commit their organizations' resources to the achievement of the goals they have set for the organization. These functions also pertain to sales executives and managers as they seek to direct the activities of their respective subunits.

In their function as chief administrators charged with building an organizational structure suitable for their chosen strategic missions, Andrews's leaders fashion a "committed organization." As chief mediators and integrators, they are responsible for the climate of their organizations, the quality of cooperation among individuals and segments of the organization, the degree to which members experience personal growth, and the effectiveness and efficiency of the work that their organizations accomplish. These leaders are ultimately responsible for task assignments, incentives, information systems, and controls. Such leaders are the final judges of the results of individual and organizational efforts. Moreover, in carrying out the functions of strategy-makers and structure-builders, chief executives are expected to be role models to those below them. Andrews says that leaders are likely to have "drive, intellectual ability, initiative, creativeness, social ability, and flexibility," but he agrees with others that there seems to be no personality mold or list of traits that can be universally ascribed to leaders.

All prominent writers suggest that leadership includes effective execution—"getting it done." Effective execution is defined as achieving goals through treating people, individually and in groups, with dignity, with respect, and in such ways as to bring out the best in them. In this view, however, the directions or goals are assumed. Later writers suggest that leadership goes beyond effective execution and includes innovation: forming the character of the organization, providing it with direction, and controlling and coordinating its group interests and conflicts.

Philip Selznick was perhaps the first author to recognize the role of innovation in leadership and to distinguish leadership from administration ("organizational engineering"). In his classic work, *Leadership in Administration* (Row, Peterson and Company, 1957), Selznick points out that administration tends to seek and reward efficiency—an operating ideal that presumes that goals have been settled and that the resources and methods for achieving them are available. Administrative activity is one of joining available means to known ends, a level of decision making Selznick calls "routine." Decisions that affect the basic character of the organization—determining the goals and developing the resources and methods for achieving those goals—he calls "critical." These latter decisions are the responsibilities of leadership.

Selznick also distinguishes between organizations and institutions. An organization is a "rational instrument," a group of people assembled to perform tasks but expendable once those tasks are accomplished. By contrast, an institution is a "natural product of social needs and pressures, a responsive, adaptive, enduring organism." Despite the popular connotation of the word, he points out that an institution has none of the pejorative overtones of a bureaucracy, whose activities are rigidly circumscribed by red tape. (Selznick's "institution" is what I call a "high-performance organization.")

Selznick's major premise is that executives, as they make the transition from administrative management to institutional leadership, begin to perform the key leadership functions, which he identifies as follows:

1. *Defining institutional mission.* This task involves understanding the true commitments of the institution as set by internal and external (environmental) demands. It is a method of setting goals that influences the mission, direction, and structure of the institution. An important aspect in determining the institution's mission is the identification and development of its "distinctive competence," the ability to do well a particular kind of work.

2. *Gaining institutional commitment.* Not only do leaders determine the course of their institutions, they also shape the institution's social structures, a phenomenon Selznick calls "the institutional embodiment of purpose." This task involves stamping the institution with distinctive ways of making decisions or with unique commitments to aims, methods, or clienteles, so that the organization as a technical instrument becomes "infused with value." These values sensitize the members of the institution to the most appropriate ways of thinking and responding, and thereby produce "understood

meanings" that ensure that both the letter and the spirit are observed as the institution's tasks are performed.

3. *Defending institutional integrity.* Leaders ensure the continuity of their institutions at levels beyond concern with mere survival. Institutional integrity depends on the leader's ability to maintain and defend both the institution's values and its identity. "Institutions do not create values, they embody them." Once values are embodied by persons within the institution, those people become attached to the institution and its way of doing things as persons, rather than as technicians performing a task. They identify themselves with the institution, a process that helps ensure that the institution will last at least as long as they do.

4. *Ordering internal conflict.* Internal interest groups form naturally in organizations, and leaders must regulate and channel the energies generated by the struggle between competing interests. Leaders never permit the mission of the institution to be seriously influenced by changes in the internal balance of power. At the same time, however, they avoid stifling genuine creative forces. On the one hand, leaders keep the consent of their constituents by permitting them wide latitude to perform effectively; on the other hand, they ensure that the institution fulfills its key commitments.

Leadership to Selznick is a blend of commitment, understanding, and determination that produces two characteristics of responsible behavior: the avoidance of opportunism and the avoidance of utopianism. He defines opportunism as the pursuit of immediate short-run advantages in a way "inadequately controlled by considerations of principle and ultimate consequences." A common manifestation of opportunism is making decisions that weaken or confuse the distinctiveness of the institution. He defines utopianism as "the avoidance of hard choices by flights to abstraction." A common manifestation of utopianism is overgeneralization of objectives. For example, he feels that the widely accepted statement of business purpose, "to make a profit," is too general to serve as a guideline for responsible decision making.

To summarize, Selznick's effective leaders steer a course for their institutions between opportunism and utopianism. He further suggests that they also evidence certain creative behavior: the transformation of groups of people from neutral, technical units into participants who have a peculiar stamp, sensitivity, and commitment. The practical result of creative behavior is that institutional goals and objectives gain spontaneous and reasoned support, not by coercion but by the free expression of accepted principles.

Selznick's ideas are relevant and pertinent to the development and maintenance of a high-performance sales force. As managers gain positions of increasing responsibility, the scope of their leadership activities widens from dealing successfully in small, face-to-face, individual and group situations to dealing successfully with larger, more complex groups of people. At the same time, the responsibility inherent in their leadership positions enlarges from accountability for the successful performance of relatively simple tasks to maintaining the continuity of whole organizations. Managing motivation depends on creative leadership.

NEWTON'S LAWS

I. The speed of the leader is the speed of the pack.

Chapter 3

Strategic Decisions

The purpose of an organization is to accomplish its mission(s) while satisfying the requirements of its various stakeholders, such as employees, stockholders, suppliers, and customers. How it chooses to define and achieve its purpose is called strategy. A strategic decision is one that has the potential to alter the future course and character of the organization. A hospital with limited financial resources, for example, may have to choose between purchasing a CAT scanner and a helicopter. The former would provide more sophisticated care and treatment to its currently served market; the latter would make available emergency care to an extended market. A university may raise money for an endowed chair to attract a distinguished scholar or for improved athletic facilities to attract better student-athletes. The former option might enhance its reputation within academic circles. The latter might enhance its reputation among alumni and the general public.

Tactical decisions, on the other hand, are made to implement strategic decisions: what brand of CAT scanner to buy or who to hire as the Don Quixote Professor of Spanish Literature. Strategic decisions tend to have an impact on the organization at a more distant point in time than do tactical decisions. Strategic decisions commit the organization to a series of planned, sequential activities. For this reason, effective sales and other senior executives are sensitive to and try to prepare for (anticipate) the ever-changing events in the environments within which their organization must exist and thrive. These events can be of a societal nature (as in the case of mores and attitudes), of a structural nature (as in the case of population and age shifts), of a political nature (as in the case of legislation or fiat), or of a technological nature (as in the case of innovation and obsolescence). In this sense, strategic decisions made by executives in high-performance organizations are proactive.

Proactive strategic decisions enable organizations to take advantage of environmental opportunities. For example, a university governing body decides to offer night programs in a distant but fast-growing metropolitan area, thus increasing its student base, its status, power, and influence, and its ability to perform its educational mission.

Strategic decisions can also be reactive. The same environmental forces that provide opportunities can also pose threats that force an organization to respond. In the face of low-cost, hand-held calculators, for example, an organization gives up manufacturing slide rules and commits resources to manufacturing surveying instruments. In the face of shifting demographics, a hospital converts to a nursing home.

In low-performance sales forces, sales executives are obsessed by the desire to solve current problems and make current things work. As a consequence, they are little interested in the future. They view change as an annoyance and seldom plan for it.

In high-performance sales forces, sales executives understand the implications of environmental events now and how those events are likely to influence the organization in the future. They respect the adage: The only constant is change. They are excited by change, they anticipate it, and they plan for it.

Strategic decisions involve a substantial commitment of an organization's resources—people, skills, technologies, facilities, relationships, reputation, and money, just to name a few. In high-performance organizations, executives develop the organization's resources so that those resources can be committed to the proper opportunities when they present themselves or can be used to respond effectively to threats when necessary. The development of an organization's resources, as with sensitivity to environmental change, requires a long-term perspective.

Clarity of mission directs the strategic process. It helps ensure that the organization and its members are doing the right things. The tactical process helps ensure that the organization and its members are doing the things right.

All organizations have options available, courses of action that they can take in pursuit of their goals. Because good strategies create more options, high-performance organizations can choose from a wider range of options than can low-performance organizations. In high-performance organizations, the opportunity to select the most desirable options from among the doable creates healthy tensions that provide employees with a climate of energy and creativity. In low-performance organizations, the opportunities to choose desirable courses of action are limited. As a consequence, the unhealthy tensions associated with limited choice—organizational learned helplessness—foster conditions that sap organizational vitality. This condition can become particularly acute within a sales force whose members all too easily can perceive themselves as "outsiders." Members of unhealthy organizations can become bored, lethargic, and consumed by "What the hell difference does it make" attitudes. Deprived of opportunities to do the right thing, they lose their natural inclination to do the thing right.

Bad strategic decisions produce an atmosphere of averting disaster and putting out fires. Good strategic decisions, well articulated, provide a business unit's members with a sense of shared purpose and a genuine commitment to fulfilling the business unit's mission.

Managing motivation for a high-performance sales force involves providing sales reps with that same sense of shared purpose and genuine commitment.

NEWTON'S LAWS

II. It takes a lot of creativity to deal with reality.

Chapter 4

Marketing Strategy

The primary responsibility of the marketing executive is to formulate marketing strategy and develop marketing plans to implement that strategy. Without a soundly conceived strategy based on thorough understanding of customer wants, the sales force will not get to first base. Put another way, the best sales force in the world will find it almost impossible to sell a product that is poorly conceived, poorly designed, poorly manufactured, poorly distributed, poorly priced, and poorly promoted. Managing sales force motivation requires managing your marketing activities.

STRATEGIC PLANNING

Marketing strategy is but one facet of a business unit's overall strategy. Formulating marketing strategy is an activity performed within the context of overall strategic planning. The latter involves (1) identifying the nature of the business by selecting specific objectives from the many possible objectives, (2) plotting the course of the business by forming plans to achieve those objectives, and

(3) determining the character of the business by describing the policies that will support those plans. This sort of planning ensures that short-term decisions advance rather than hinder long-range goals.

Strategic planning begins with identifying risks and opportunities in the environment. This assessment requires data on current economic, social, and political conditions, as well as reasonable predictions about those conditions 2, 10, even 20 years in the future. Executives try to answer such questions as: Will interest rates continue to rise? Will skilled labor be available? Will workers prefer shorter hours to higher salaries? Will local governments become more active in regulating businesses? Will the federal government's policies foster economic growth?

In addition to predicting general economic and social conditions, strategic planning attempts to forecast factors that are particularly pertinent to the business. Sample questions posed about these factors include:

☐ Will the predicted increase in retired persons in the United States offer us new product opportunities?

☐ Will increased leisure time bring similar opportunities?

☐ Will our current competitors remain strong?

☐ Will our technologies be rendered obsolete by new processes?

☐ Will our competitors spend more of their funds on advertising or on expanding their distribution networks?

After analysis of the risks and opportunities in the environment, strategic planning involves projecting the resources that the business unit will need to seize the opportunities and minimize the risks. Internal resources must be evaluated and plans made to secure or develop additional resources as needed. Such resources include personnel, finances, facilities, the firm's reputation, and its relationships with suppliers and customers.

To develop marketing strategy, you follow the same basic format as strategic planners: match the environmental opportunities—potential customers—with the firm's resources—current and future offerings.

MARKET SEGMENTATION

For every product, potential groups of customers must be identified so that marketing efforts can be targeted efficiently and effectively toward those groups. Identifying potential customers requires, first, that one understand what motivates consumers to buy the product. How do people decide what goods and services to buy?

One useful theory about consumer decision making holds that customers are guided by their perceptions of the functional and the symbolic qualities of the product. A customer chooses a product not only for the product's intrinsic value as the customer perceives it, but also for the product's ability to enhance the purchaser's feelings of self-worth. The functional aspect of buying a carpet, for instance, might involve an assessment of product durability: Will it wear well? The symbolic aspect might involve an assessment of style: What will the neighbors think of this shade? Similarly, in industrial marketing, a purchasing agent might be concerned with a functional attribute: Will this lathe be easy to service? The purchasing agent might also be concerned with a symbolic attribute: How will the user feel about operating a lathe manufactured overseas?

How do customers evaluate the functional and symbolic characteristics of a product? Some rely entirely on their own judgments. Most people find such independence too risky, however. To temper the risk of making incorrect choices, some people rely on certain brands, some rely on certain vendors, others rely on selections made by social reference groups. These groups may subtly determine, for example, the success of an L. L. Bean chamois-cloth shirt or a Brooks Brothers gray pin-striped suit. Successful marketing,

then, gains customers by developing their brand and vendor loyal-
ties, by providing functional information, and by offering symbolic
reassurance. Successful marketing builds the foundation for successful selling.

After you have determined the most likely functional and symbolic
needs that the product fulfills, the second step in developing marketing strategy is to isolate the groups of customers that are most
likely to have those particular functional and symbolic needs. The
process of defining customer groups is called market segmentation.

Demographic analysis is the most common means of segmenting
the market. Groups are identified by sex, age, residence, income,
and so on. Objective data are often insufficient, however, to determine consumer buying habits. Thus many executives supplement
demographic data with an analysis of buyers' motivations. This
kind of analysis has become known as psychographic segmentation
and includes such criteria for identifying customer groups as the
customer's perception of value, his or her susceptibility to change,
the purpose in purchasing the product, aesthetic preferences, consumption behavior, and general self-confidence and familiarity with
the product class.

The beer industry provides numerous illustrations of psychographic
segments. Beer drinkers can be distinguished by their purposes in
drinking the product—refreshment, stimulation, or sociability.
They can be distinguished by their aesthetic preferences for "light"
or for "full-bodied" beer. Another criterion is the consumer's perception of value. Some people want to pay the lowest possible price for
their beer; others are willing to pay more for "premium" beer. And
some will pay even more for the unusual flavor or snob appeal of an
import. The market can also be segmented by consumption habits.
Beer drinkers may drink occasionally, frequently, or both frequently and in large quantities.

Successful segmentation requires four conditions. First is the identification of a group or groups of customers with similar product
interests or needs. Ideally, this activity should produce a more
imaginative, and therefore unique, grouping of customers, than

simply blanketing the market regardless of whether the identification is done demographically, psychographically, or in combination.

Second, the target segments must contain enough potential buyers to be profitable relative to the business unit's commitment of financial and other resources. You may have the best widget in the world, but if it only appeals to a handful of people, you are going to lose a lot of money trying to market it.

Third, the target segments must be accessible to the business unit's sales force and promotional activities. Some industries (the educational market with its plethora of school boards, for instance) are so scattered, so complex in their decision-making processes, and so politically unpredictable that only business units with large sales forces and huge advertising and promotion budgets care to risk marketing to them. Some are actually markets within markets, each requiring different products with different marketing approaches.

Finally, the target segments should be defensible. Once established, your business unit's position should be difficult to dislodge. Efforts should be concentrated on maintaining and increasing customer satisfaction and product superiority. An identifiable niche represents a rewarding target to your sales force. A defensible niche is the closest thing to a monopoly.

PRODUCT POSITIONING

Matching characteristics of the product to a particular market segment is known as product positioning. An example of product positioning is a major breakfast cereal marketer that developed the first "nutritional" ready-to-eat cereal marketed nationally in the United States. Despite two powerful competitors, it maintained its dominant share of the market segment most appropriate to the product's specifications: It was the least filling, least fattening, and least sweet of the three new cereals. Company executives decided that these characteristics would suit adult purchasers, and its advertising was consistently aimed at this market segment. By contrast, the advertising campaigns for its competitors were inconsistent. Some were aimed at adults; others at children. Some stressed taste, some nutrition, and some economy. Credit for the innovator's success must certainly be shared with its advertising agency, but advertising people find it easier to be creative for clients who know exactly what their goals are.

The advantages of good product positioning are numerous. The company's manufacturing resources are committed to salable products. Decisions to abbreviate or to extend the product lines are based on the needs of identified groups of customers, not merely on manufacturing ease or research and development breakthroughs. Advertising copy appeals to the pertinent attributes of potential customers. Advertising media are selected to reach specific consumer groups, an approach more effective and inexpensive than that of choosing media at random. Pricing decisions are based partly on the prices that customers are willing to pay. Distribution decisions are based on customers' vendor preferences and service expectations. Sales executives can identify likely customers in advance and can provide their sales reps with more effective sales aids and training programs.

PURCHASING BEHAVIOR

Although people may later regret doing something, at the moment they did it, they perceived themselves as behaving rationally—although that behavior may not appear so to someone else. The same holds true with purchasing behavior. Whether rational or not, the particular actions taken by a buyer in making a purchase decision are his or her way to solve a problem. Some purchase decisions can produce complex actions and time-consuming behavior; others can produce simple, almost reflexive behavior. Some purchase decisions can be characterized as having high degrees of personal involvement; others by low degrees of personal involvement. Figure 2 shows some examples.

FIGURE 2

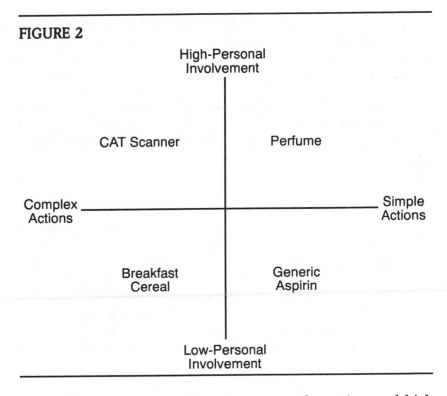

The upper left quadrant of the figure—complex actions and high involvement—includes big-ticket purchases that require a lot of data gathering and analysis to avoid making a big mistake. The lower left quadrant—complex actions and low involvement—includes purchases that induce variety-seeking behavior. The upper right quadrant—simple actions and high involvement—includes purchases that are so important and difficult to assess that buying behavior is reduced to dependence on a favorite or heavily advertised brand. The lower right quadrant—simple actions and low involvement—includes products with little differentiation and negligible risk to the purchaser, such as commodities.

The placement of a product or service in one of these quadrants does not depend on product characteristics and attributes but rather on the purchaser's personal characteristics and attributes. Some people don't seek variety in their breakfast cereals. Some people pay little attention to the prestige of their perfume. Some people will skip the analyses of specifications and order the "leading brand" of CAT scanner. Some people prefer brand-name aspirin to generic because they believe in giving themselves the best.

A number of theories attempt to explain complex decision processes. The following one is a combination of the ideas of Philip Kotler of Northwestern University and Donald Cox and Raymond Bauer of Harvard University.

Motive

A need once recognized becomes a motive, a force that influences a person's behavior. Much marketing effort is directed toward making people aware that they need something—a statement particularly relevant to new products. Much sales activity is directed toward persuading prospective buyers that they need something "our product" offers. When need awareness is insufficient, the sales rep usually hears the prospect reject the product by saying something self-centered like, "I don't need it," "We can't afford it," or "I'll think it over."

Criteria

When the motive to buy has been established, most prospective buyers begin a search for information. To put this information in perspective and to understand better the tradeoffs involved in evaluating product specifications, prospects usually begin determining their buying criteria with such questions as these:

☐ What should I be looking for in this product?

☐ What are the tradeoffs between attribute A and attribute B?

☐ Do I really need attribute C?

☐ Is attribute D worth X dollars?

☐ Are there any other attributes I should be considering?

Many sales reps overlook this critical stage in the buying decision, because they assume that prospects are ready to evaluate the merits of particular product attributes before the prospects have become convinced of the relevance of those attributes to their particular needs. When criteria are insufficiently formulated, the sales rep usually hears the prospect say something to gain time—such as, "Can you call back later?" "I'll have to check with Engineering," or "Leave your spec sheets and I'll look 'em over when I get a chance."

Specifications

Once prospective buyers have determined their buying criteria—the relative importance of the various attributes and the tradeoffs involved—they are ready to continue their search for information. This time, however, the search centers on collecting and comparing data that help them develop those product specifications that satisfy their particular criteria. For some people, certain specifications are essential; that is, "If it doesn't have four-wheel drive, I don't want it." For other people certain specifications are nonessential: "I'd really like four-wheel drive, but if the truck has a lot of cargo space and the price is right, I can live without it."

The attempt to influence prospects' specifications is an important part of sales reps' jobs, whether they be retail clerks ("I think you'll like this one better") or sales engineers ("Our model delivers 400 more horsepower than our competitor's model, which means quicker response from the control panel and finer cutting tolerances for you"). When the product specifications don't match the prospect's specifications, the sales rep usually hears the prospect say something about the product, such as: "It's not fast enough," "It's too expensive," or "It doesn't fit into our plans."

Decision

Once prospective buyers have compared their desired specifications with the various product offerings (clusters of attributes), the search for information is over and the buyers are ready to make a decision, "rational" or not. At this point, two factors can interfere with the consummation of the sale.

The first is external to the purchaser and has to do with the marketplace: The product is out-of-stock or discontinued; a new product is on the market and needs evaluation; another product has come out at a lower price; a consumer magazine has given the product a bad rating. The second is internal to the purchaser and has to do with the buyer's self-confidence and perception of risk. If buyer self-confidence is low, either in general or specific to this particular situation because the decision process to date has left the buyer feeling uneasy, the risk the buyer perceives can be intolerably high.

The perceived risk comes in two forms—product risk and purchase risk. Product risk raises the question, "Is this product a good buy?" and involves issues such as: Will it work? Will it last? Is it worth the money? To reduce product risk, many buyers undertake a last-minute search for additional information. Purchase risk raises the question, "Am I being a good buyer?" and involves such issues as: What will the boss think? Am I being foolish? Can I afford it? To reduce purchase risk, many buyers will undertake a last-minute search for reassurance. Even if given the opportunity to become involved in a buyer's decision (in contrast to being involved in the decision process) a sales rep will seldom get anywhere supplying information to reduce purchase risk (what will the boss think?) or reassurance to reduce product risk (will it work?).

Dissonance

In many instances the decision to buy produces a lot of postpurchase tension in the buyer. This phenomenon is particularly in evidence if the risk, either product or purchase, is still perceived as high. Many successful business units attempt to reduce buyer dissonance by providing postpurchase information and reassurance to their customers through personal sales calls and other follow-up activities. Sales reps who fail to follow through on their obligations to reduce postpurchase dissonance may be eroding valuable relationships.

ADVERTISING

If the success of your sales force depends on the quality and quantity of your business unit's advertising and if your customers need presale information or postsale reassurance about your products and services, you should be paying a lot of attention to your business unit's decision-making process about advertising. Better still, you should become an active participant in that process.

The *effectiveness* of your advertising message with potential customers depends heavily on the talents of creative people, guided by information about your markets, products, and marketing objectives. The *efficiency* of your advertising campaign refers to its benefits to the company—that is, its ability to increase sales at reasonable advertising costs.

Advertising is more likely to be effective if your customers perceive both the functional and symbolic risks of adopting your product to be relatively minor. If, on the other hand, your customers are particularly anxious for your product to fulfill its promises, they are likely to turn from advertising to more credible sources of information and reassurance. For example, consider two products that are similar in composition and use but differ in customer risk perception. The first product is an athlete's foot powder; the second a medicated baby powder used to control diaper rash. Customers for the first product may prefer not to bother seeing a physician and may be too embarrassed to ask a pharmacist or a friend for advice. Moreover, the risk that the product will not work may not seem significant. Thus, these customers are willing to rely on information conveyed by advertisements. On the other hand, purchasers of a medicated baby powder, anxious for the product to relieve the baby's discomfort immediately, will probably rely on information from pediatricians or other trusted sources, such as grandmothers. For these customers, advertising will have relatively little credibility.

Advertising's effectiveness is also determined by product characteristics. In his classic work, *The Economic Effects of Advertising*, Neil H. Borden identified five conditions under which advertising is most likely to be effective. The first condition occurs when there is growing primary demand for the product. Athletic footwear is a good example. But once consumers lose interest in the product category as a whole, advertising campaigns are unlikely to turn the tide. Once men stopped wearing hats (thanks to President Kennedy), no single hatmaker's advertisements could generate much business.

The second condition occurs when the product allows high-gross margins that can pay for large dollar investments in advertising. Pain relievers typically have high margins. Salt does not.

The third condition occurs when the product's qualities are hard to inspect at point of purchase. For example, in the case of mattresses, power drills, or packaged goods, customers are forced to rely on the manufacturer's or the brand's reputation—which usually has been communicated through advertising.

The fourth condition occurs when the product can be easily associated with a symbol central to the potential customer's self-image—for example, the Marlboro Man or Lauren Hutton for Revlon cosmetics.

The final condition occurs when products are clearly differentiated from one another. Creative people can develop more stimulating advertisements for products with truly distinctive features than the creative staff can for products with only symbolic advantages.

Pet foods are a prime example of an advertisable product. First, the number of pets is increasing faster than the number of people. Second, gross margins (I am told) are enormous because the ingredients—horsemeat and/or grains—are cheap. Third, the stuff usually comes in cans or bags that defy inspection at point-of-sale (you wouldn't want to be seen tasting it anyway). Fourth, kittens and puppies make marvelous symbols. Finally, although the products probably taste pretty much the same to the pets, the possibilities of differentiation by using anthropomorphic appeals are apparently limitless.

What are some reasons that industrial marketers tend to rely more on "push" tactics (reliance on marketing efforts to move products through the channels of distribution) than on "pull" tactics (reliance on marketing efforts to draw products through the channels of distribution)?

☐ Many industrial products do not conform well to Borden's notion of advertisability. Many are "big ticket" items, and are of keen interest to purchasing agents and users (who may not be the same individual).

☐ These big-ticket items seldom have the high-gross margins characteristic of most consumer packaged goods.

☐ Technical specifications of many industrial products afford the prospective buyer a means of comparing and contrasting one vendor's product features with those from another vendor at the point of purchase.

☐ Most industrial products cannot be invested with a symbol "central to a customer's self-image."

☐ The kinds of product differentiation activities common in industrial marketing are usually easier to explain and communicate via sales reps than via advertisements.

Nevertheless, advertising can and does play a role for many industrial products, particularly when they have characteristics similar to packaged goods. Moreover, industrial marketers find advertising messages an effective means for establishing a favorable image for their company and its sales force, for making announcements about new products, for reaching executive levels beyond those ordinarily reached through normal sales-call patterns, and for achieving a wide variety of specific communication objectives related to the product line.

Don't allow others to suggest that advertising effectiveness should be measured by changes in sales volume. Advertising is essentially a means of communication. Thus, it should be evaluated according to its ability to deliver a message. Advertising shares the responsibility for building sales volume with a host of other variables, including product policy, distribution, pricing, and—of course—the sales force.

Take, for example, an advertising campaign that makes large numbers of people aware of and favorably disposed toward a particular product. If the customer gets to the store and the product is poorly displayed, difficult to find, or out of stock, the customer may settle for a competitor's product. Even if the product is readily available, the customer may choose the competitor's product for its more attractive package, special features, lower price, or promotional offer. If the sale goes to the competitor, it wasn't the advertising that was responsible.

The key to advertising efficiency is clear-cut objectives. An example of such an objective is "to increase the proportion of potential buyers who are aware of our unconditional guarantee from the current 30 percent to 50 percent by the end of the year." The chosen advertising objective should be achievable within the chosen time limit, and it should fit into the firm's overall marketing objectives. The objective should also have a built-in criterion for measuring the campaign's performance. And here is where efficiency and effectiveness become intertwined. The objective in the example here uses the criterion of customer awareness, readily measured by assessing consumers' memories of information presented in current advertisements. Two other common measures of advertising effectiveness used in setting advertising objectives are consumer attitudes and consumer behavior. Changes in attitudes can be measured by determining changes in consumers' stated preferences for the product. Changes in consumer behavior can be measured by counting such indicators as store visits, requests for brochures, and use of coupons.

If your advertising campaign has clear-cut objectives, you can ascribe a dollar value to the achievement of those objectives. For example, having established an objective of increasing consumer awareness of the unconditional guarantee from 30 percent to 50 percent, you can test consumer awareness when the campaign is over, calculate the costs of that change, and compare it to the dollar value ascribed to the achievement of that objective.

Advertising objectives tend to vary with the stage of a product's life cycle:

1. In the introductory stage, advertising can make customers aware that the product exists and educate them about its use.

2. In the growth stage, when firms vie for customer preference by offering functional variations, advertising can emphasize the advantages of the product's particular cluster of features.

3. In the mature and declining stages, as competing products become increasingly similar, advertising can emphasize symbolic differences rather than functional ones.

In these latter two stages, some criticize advertising for influencing customers with "irrational" appeals. Such activity is often necessary, however, to sustain sales among essentially similar products and generate sufficient profits to enable the launch of new products. Indeed, if the products are that similar in performance and cost, it doesn't matter which one the consumer chooses to buy. In the declining stage, when the products are essentially identical and the customers are highly sophisticated, if not bored, advertising is often used to keep the distribution channels reassured that the firm still supports the product.

There is nothing mysterious about advertising. If you don't know why you're using it, however, advertising is simply an expense, not a tool to help your sales force achieve your business unit's objectives.

DISTRIBUTION

If the success of your sales force depends on where and under what conditions your products and services are offered for sale, you should be paying a lot of attention to how your business-unit decisions move products and services from point to point and how your channels of distribution—collectively known as "the trade"—are selected and managed.

Physical distribution involves choosing basic units of shipment, methods of transport, and storage systems. Once a physical distribution system has been set up, changes in trade or consumer buying patterns may show the need for changes in material handling, inventory levels, stocking points, data processing, or transport methods. The costs of making such changes must be weighed against the anticipated gains in customer satisfaction and trade cooperation.

You should be included in the business unit's deliberations on these issues if possible. Don't be handcuffed by some accountant! Because physical distribution is influenced by many nonmarketing factors, such as plant location and manufacturing technology, however, it may not be possible for you to become involved. In fact, in many firms, physical distribution is assigned to manufacturing rather than to marketing executives.

In selecting distribution channels and policies, you should keep in mind two basic premises. First, customers seek dealers whose physical facilities or business practices are congruent with the customers' self-images. (For simplicity's sake, the term *dealers* refers here to wholesalers, distributors, jobbers, retailers, and other types of intermediary agents.) Your dealers should fit the image your customers prefer. Second, your dealers should match the characteristics of each of your particular products—regardless of whether these dealers handle your other products. For example, a new product may require special promotions or services that cannot be delivered by your usual channels. If the product represents an unusual degree of purchasing risk to the customer, choose dealers who can educate customers and reduce the perceived risk. Similarly, if the product requires extensive promotion to make its claims heard above those of competitors or requires special installation or postsale service, choose dealers equipped to perform those activities. If the product's cost is high or if large volumes must be held in the dealer's inventory, choose dealers with the requisite financial resources.

Your dealers are extensions of your business unit, not outsiders, enemies, or even customers. They should work in tandem with your sales force. If, in arrogance or carelessness, your business-unit personnel provoke or allow the dealer to gain greater strength in the local market than you have, you will lose control over the dealer, that market, and (eventually) your brand. The rise of the so-called generics—a phenomenon that has spread from pharmaceuticals to household food staples to industrial goods—is a good example.

Like advertising, distribution decisions must take into account the varying phases of the product's life cycle. In the introductory stage, dealers are generally selected for their abilities to perform certain key functions. They must be able to guide the customer to a favorable first experience with the product, to monitor the customer's experience with the product, and to provide postsale service, if necessary. Usually, the best distribution system for the introductory stage is direct and exclusive, for several reasons. Intermediate agents are not yet necessary, because the small volumes moving from point of production to point of sale do not require sophisticated logistics. Direct distribution gives you control over the customer's first experience with the product and rapid, accurate information about that first experience. Direct contact with the reseller also enables you to explain the product and its use to all parties.

Exclusive distribution—using one or two dealers in a given trading area or market—is desirable for both you and the dealer at this stage. Dealers can support the product more fully when other dealers carry no competing items or product lines. In return, you help the dealers to promote the product, to train sales and service personnel, to carry adequate inventory, and to react quickly to customer inquiries and complaints.

In the growth stage, you are in a race for additional dealers. Exclusivity in distribution gives way to selectivity. Competitors at this stage try to get their product lines carried by the "best" dealers, whether or not these merchants carry competing lines. Eventually, selective distribution is replaced by intensive distribution as competitors try to have their products carried by all dealers that customers consider appropriate for their products.

If you were the original innovator, you now face a dilemma. Do you keep the promise of "protected sales territories" and thereby risk losing market share and perhaps double-crossing from dealers who eventually take on competing lines anyway? Or do you break the promise, jettison the policy of exclusivity, and join your competitors in the scramble for broader distribution?

Some companies handle this dilemma by introducing additional lines under new brand names—preserving the original brand for the original dealers and using the new brands for additional dealers. Sometimes the new brands are identical in quality, appearance, and price to the original brand. More often, the new brand is lower in price and quality, as may befit a less exclusive dealer network.

In the mature stage, lack of product differentiation and increasing customer sophistication mean that your dealers' service and sales capabilities are usually no longer as useful or as cost effective as before. Your focus may now shift from intensive distribution to mass distribution. Competitors in this stage try to have their products carried by all possible dealers, whether or not customers may initially have considered those vendors to be appropriate. Inexpensive cameras are sold in supermarkets, light bulbs in drugstores, and clock-radios in bookstores. Mass distribution means indirect distribution. Middlemen proliferate, because intermediate stocking points are needed to ensure quick responses to dwindling inventories. You no longer have much control over the vendor. Only for the most complex or high-priced products is controlling the channels still necessary or cost effective.

In the declining stage, mass distribution reaches its extreme limits. If the product's characteristics permit, your sales reps may be replaced by vending machines.

If your distribution decisions are good ones and your channels receive the attention they deserve, conditions exist for your sales force to achieve its maximum potential. If, however, your decisions are poor and your channels are neglected, the best sales force in the world is going to have trouble doing justice to your product line.

PRICING

If selling your products and services at the right price is important to the success of your sales force, you better take a lot of interest in how your business-unit marketers and accountants go about the task of pricing. Better still, get involved.

What price should you charge for a new product? The easiest way is to apply a uniform markup on costs, but this approach does not allow you to charge premium prices in good times or charge low prices to stimulate volume during hard times. As an innovator, you enjoy a pricing latitude that will never recur. The customer has no experience with your product. No competition exists. And, depending on your product's novelty, its benefits have not been translated into a specific price range.

In this situation, you can choose a high price relative to costs. This pricing policy, known as skimming, has some obvious advantages. It enables you to recoup your investment quickly. It also helps you to minimize the loss if demand falls short of expectations or to maximize profits if the product's life cycle turns out to be short. High prices are particularly useful for products with patent protection (such as the early photocopiers) or long production lead times (such as commercial jet aircraft). Skimming is also effective with products that are drastic departures from current offerings and whose pricing may require experimentation before the most acceptable long-run price level can be determined. You can always reduce the price when competition enters the market.

On the other hand, offering the product at an initially low price also has advantages, particularly if the financial resources exist to ride out a long period of losses or marginal profits. This pricing strategy, called penetration, uses low prices to build market share while discouraging competition from entering your market. By the time competitors recognize the potential profits of your new market, their promotional efforts to catch up primarily serve to expand the market that you dominate.

Penetration pricing makes particular sense when the product's life cycle is expected to be long (Henry Ford knew what he was doing when he priced the Model A). It is also useful when unit costs are expected to drop considerably with increases in volume and when you wish to protect your hold on the market against anticipated strong competition. The firm producing the most units usually enjoys the lowest cost of value added per unit. This phenomenon, called the experience curve, means, of course, that the firm with the largest market share should be the low-cost producer. The experience curve is a strong argument for building market share rapidly through penetration pricing.

Whether you decide to price high or low, the key consideration with a new product is to get it accepted in the marketplace. Novelty often means ambiguity. If the targeted audience can readily evaluate the product's benefits, a high price may be justifiable. On the other hand, if the product's features, benefits, and uses are difficult for customers to grasp, a high price may deter its acceptance.

In the growth stage of the product's life cycle, you begin to lose pricing latitude. As competition focuses on product features, customers begin to weigh the benefits of features against their costs. The question in the customer's mind changes from "Should I buy a CD player?" to "If I buy a CD player, is remote control worth an extra $50?" At this point, product differentiation breeds brand preferences—preferences that you hope will carry over into the mature stage, where the differentiation is less marked.

Thus, in the growth stage, price emerges as an important element of the brand's and the product's identity. The overriding pricing consideration in this stage is to set price ranges that can be justified by functional improvements.

In the mature stage, products are fairly similar. Your pricing lati-tude is now restricted not only by consumer sophistication but per-haps also by the increasing complexity of the channels of distribu-tion. The longer the chain—agents, wholesalers, jobbers, distributors, retailers—the more their margins add up. You must now decide whether to make the product's price the basis of compe-tition. Can you increase market share and/or profitability by reduc-ing prices relative to those of competitors? Or would other market-ing tactics—such as increased advertising, broader distribution, or better customer service—be more effective?

In some cases, conditions within your industry will determine whether you choose to compete by price. Price competition among mature products can be dampened if (1) product differentiation is still feasible (as with cameras); (2) symbolic values can still be created (as with cosmetics); (3) customers cannot easily gauge the benefits of a particular brand (as with dog food); or (4) customers cannot easily compare brands (as with prescription drugs). On the other hand, price competition becomes intense under the following conditions:

☐ One or more firms can offer customers a clear choice between low price and brand reputation (as with rental cars).

☐ The trade is more powerful than the manufacturers and can offer low-priced, private-label brands.

☐ The industry faces competition from substitute products (alumi-num competing with steel).

The decision whether to compete by price also depends on your perceptions of future conditions in the market. How will general economic conditions such as interest rates and consumer confidence influence demand? How many competitors will enter or leave the market? Will a price leader emerge?

Determining whether to compete on the basis of price also depends on consumer attitudes regarding your product. Is there enough dif-ferentiation in your product to warrant a price premium or at least to ward off any need to reduce the price? Does a residue of loyalty exist from previous marketing activities that will insulate you from your competitors' pricing tactics? Are customers' choices in this product class determined solely by price, or are customers influenced by other factors?

Finally, the decision to engage in price competition depends on your business-unit objectives. What role is this product expected to play among the firm's other lines? Has the product been selected to promote some image of quality or price for the line as a whole? Is the product expected to generate profits to support other products? Or is it a "loss leader," priced for volume sales in order to attract customers to more profitable lines?

Whether or not price competition becomes the dominant pricing strategy, you may decide to use tactical pricing—temporary price changes made to achieve specific marketing objectives. One type of tactical pricing is trade loading—offering dealers special discounts (called buying allowances) to purchase specified quantities within a specified time period. To move products out of the stores, you may try trade unloading, offering dealers discounts to display the product prominently or offering advertising allowances for products featured in the dealer's advertising.

Consumer loading is often used simultaneously with trade unloading. Common forms of consumer loading are the "cents-off" deal and the "one-free-with-five" deal. Once the products have been purchased, consumer unloading encourages immediate consumption. For example, you can insert cents-off coupons inside the package. Such tactical pricing maneuvers are used most often in the product's mature or declining phase.

The common tactical-pricing equivalents in industrial marketing are push money, also called PMs and spiffs, and a variety of incentives in the form of contests and special promotions to dealers and their sales reps. Push money is generally paid to dealer sales reps on a per-unit-sold basis to encourage them to sell one brand rather than another.

In the declining phase of a product's life cycle, the competing brands are all equivalent, if not identical, and you are rarely able to charge a price premium. Nor are you able to reduce prices significantly. Prices are already so low as to allow only the barest margins. Your task is to find the lowest price that will yield a reasonable profit. The keys to success in this stage are low-cost production, mass distribution to increase sales volume, and minimal expenditures on advertising and promotion.

Pricing is a critical judgment call. Too few sales executives pay enough attention to it. The best sales force in the world is going to have a difficult time selling products and services at prices inconsistent with potential customers' definitions of value.

PRODUCT POLICY

If the success of your sales force depends on the qualities and desirability of your product offerings, you should be paying a lot of attention to how your business-unit decisions regarding product policy are made and implemented, and you should get personally involved in helping to make those decisions.

Product policy refers to the choice of features and associations that are secondary to the basic product. Forming product policy includes determining the product's design, appearance, and packaging; choosing the variations to be offered within the product line, such as various styles, colors, and sizes; and determining whether the product will be branded to link it with other products marketed by the firm.

When the product is in its introductory phase, its novelty is often the key impediment to consumer acceptance. In some cases, novelty causes customers to question the product's functional value. Power brakes and power steering, for example, required drivers to learn new driving habits, and many drivers complained that the innovations were unnecessary and dangerous. Word processors were initially resisted by many secretaries. Microwave ovens also initially seemed risky and unlikely to work as well as old-fashioned ovens. For other new products, symbolic attributes are uncertain. Molded plastic furniture initially seemed of questionable aesthetic value.

Generally, you are best advised to choose for the initial introduction the model that is most likely to provide customers with a favorable first experience with the product. In addition to selecting features and variations for the product, product policy in the introductory stage includes determining the proper fit between the new product and others already marketed by the firm. The key question here is whether the sales of both old and new products will be helped or hindered by the association. Giving the new product an already established brand name may help its sales. On the other hand, if the new product has quality-control problems, the new product may hurt the established brand's reputation. And if the new product's use is similar (or will be perceived as similar) to that of an older product, one of the two products may draw sales from (cannibalize) the other product. If you believe that cannibalization is a significant risk, you may choose product features to minimize the similarity between the two products. The advertising, pricing, and distribution methods may also be varied for each product to reduce the risk of cannibalization.

In the growth stage, when the innovator's product has become accepted in the marketplace, success attracts adapters, firms that develop variations on the original model. Accumulated product variations and improvements combine with the sheer mass of promotional spending and sales-force effort to produce rapid growth in per-capita consumption (also known as primary demand). The new competitors capitalize on the innovator's marketing and production efforts and may profit by the innovator's technical and marketing mistakes. To survive in this stage, the innovator must offer more and better variations on the original product. The innovator can then take advantage of the increased demand that has been caused, in part, by competitors' advertising dollars and sales-force efforts.

The key product-policy decision at this stage is to choose the product features and variations that offer the best functional improvements over competitors' products. For example, many ice cream manufacturers sustained their early sales by increasing the number of flavors. In addition, branching out into frozen yogurt (once perceived as a threat), ice cream manufacturers have substantially increased the frequency and thus the overall volume of consumption.

Executives of one company have used similar methods to lengthen the product life cycle of transparent adhesive tape. To raise sales among current users, they developed a variety of dispensers that made the product easier to use. Product variations included colored, patterned, water-proofed, invisible, and write-on tapes. They introduced a similar product but one lower in price; developed a line of commercial cellophane tapes of various widths, lengths, and strengths; and developed products such as double-coated tape and reflecting tape, which used the basic material in new ways.

In the mature stage, the growth rate in per-capita consumption has begun to slow. This stage is not as profitable as the growth stage, primarily because marketing expenses increase. Product variations with genuine functional benefits have been adopted by all competitors, "gladiators" for market-share points. Because the products are now essentially similar, customers are quite sophisticated in making judgments about the relative functional value of competing brands. Generally you can use two product policies to interest customers in your products in this stage.

One policy is to augment the product's auxiliary services—offering longer warranty periods or more comprehensive service packages, for example. A second policy is to emphasize the symbolic differences between one's own and the competing products. For example, the one cigarette offers a modest functional variation—a somewhat smaller diameter than that of the average cigarette—but this product variation supported an advertising campaign that produced powerful symbolic associations for the product as a feminine cigarette. Who can confuse the "You've come a long way, baby" cigarette with any other?

In the declining stage, per-capita consumption is falling, usually because of competition from a new technology (for example, the slide rule falling prey to the hand-held calculator). Because products made by the survivors are nearly identical in function, image, and price, the only way to maintain profits is to cut costs through mass production and mass distribution. Thus, the key product-policy decision in this stage is to determine the features and associations that will enable the product to be mass produced and mass distributed at the lowest possible cost.

The best sales force in the world is going to have difficulty selling products that are ill-conceived, ill-designed, and unmatched to customer desires and preferences. High-performance sales organizations are supported by marketing executives who believe that the factory mentality of marketing makable products must be replaced by the market-driven mentality of making marketable products.

Peter Drucker, author, teacher, and business philosopher, is a giant in my profession. His dictum below—my third law—should be posted in every office, manufacturing plant, service facility, and board room in the world. It should be tattooed on the back of your hand and of the hand of everyone reporting to you.

NEWTON'S LAWS

III. The purpose of a business is to create a customer.

Drucker

Chapter 5

Desired Sales-Force Behavior

Anyone who has spent time observing sales reps from different companies as they make their sales calls will appreciate that defining their activities as "selling" is a vast oversimplification. Selling is much more than merely asking for the order. Sales activities can range from "hand holding" to pressuring the customer to buy; from long, involved negotiations with numerous customer "influentials" to door-to-door canvassing; from making highly technical presentations to sophisticated customers to haggling over price on bulk items that are purchased on a regular basis. Within the same industry, sales reps selling practically identical products to similar classes of customers will exhibit different selling behavior. This variety of activity is, or ought to be, a function of the role assigned to the sales force within the business unit's marketing strategy, not a function of how sales reps think they ought to behave. If sales reps believe that they are in business for themselves, you will have as many marketing strategies as you have sales reps.

In high-performance sales forces, therefore, executives begin with a clear understanding of the specifics of desired behavior, and they don't sidestep this necessary analytical task by describing sales-force activities in generalizations such as "They are paid to sell." Overgeneralization may cause you to ignore sales-force activities that are vital to your marketing strategy.

The first step in determining desired behavior is understanding your marketing strategy. For some sales executives, this first step is more difficult than it sounds. Sometimes unfamiliarity with marketing strategy arises from an inability to participate with marketing executives in formulating strategy. This nonparticipation can lead to a misunderstanding of how the business unit has chosen to compete, which in turn leads to a lack of commitment to marketing objectives and the improper direction of field sales activities.

Sometimes this lack of participation is caused by the formal organization itself. Reporting relationships may inhibit communication between sales and marketing personnel. Furthermore, sales and marketing personnel often have different backgrounds and personalities. Marketing executives tend to be analytical, to have formal educations in business administration, and to talk in a language of their own, using terms such as *positioning, segmentation,* and *gross rating points.* Many sales executives, on the other hand, are people who have made their marks as sales reps, have less formal business training, and are more at ease when taking a customer to lunch than when analyzing quantitative data. Most firms' methods of evaluating performance reinforce these differences: marketing executives are frequently evaluated in terms of profitability and return on investment; sales executives are more frequently evaluated in terms of sales volume.

Sales executives who are able to make useful contributions to strategy formulation are the ones who are familiar with marketing concepts and terminology. Some organizations help sales executives to achieve this familiarity through management-development programs; other organizations use a career path that gives promising sales reps positions in marketing early in their careers. By the same token, some organizations insist on sales experience before giving marketing executives positions of greater responsibility. It is as important for the marketing strategist to understand the realities of the marketplace as seen through the eyes of a sales rep as it is for the sales executive to understand how the business unit has chosen to compete.

Sales executives must also keep up with subtle shifts in marketing strategy that affect desired sales-force behavior. Nearly all business units modify their marketing strategy from year to year. Prices are changed, dealers are added or dropped, new products are featured, new advertising campaigns are begun, and so on. Every time you modify your strategy, you inexorably modify the desired behavior of your sales force. Even though these modifications are minor, over time they add up. Most marketing and sales executives, if they were to examine their marketing plans of five years ago, would be surprised at the difference between those plans and their plans for this year. Similarly, if these executives were to examine in detail what specific activities were required of the sales rep five years ago, they would be surprised at the differences in their activities today.

For example, one company I know incorporated some subtle changes in its product line several years ago and decided to reduce its volume with smaller customers and increase its volume with more profitable, larger customers. As marketing efforts toward the larger customers intensified, sales executives found themselves with obsolete call standards, badly aligned sales territories, and a sales force largely ill equipped to explain new-product benefits to the more sophisticated purchasers. Furthermore, many field sales managers were uncertain about the company's new sales emphasis and were continuing to coach and direct salespeople to call on the older, smaller accounts instead of training them to be more effective with purchasing agents. As you might expect, it took several years to straighten out the mess.

Before any policies can be instituted to encourage desired behavior and any supervisory activities can be instituted to help the sales reps to achieve it, sales executives must know what that desired behavior is. If that behavior does not have a foundation in marketing strategy, your sales force will not get to second base. If that behavior is not guided by clearly defined objectives, your sales force will end up in left field.

OBJECTIVES

As mentioned earlier, whether a sales force is blessed with high or low performance depends heavily on whether the people who define the sales-force tasks know where the business unit should be going and how best it should get there. Some executives allow their organizations to drift aimlessly, with no real sense of direction other than seizing opportunity and gaining a series of short-run advantages. Other executives define the mission of their organization clearly, gain the commitment of its members to achieving the organization's mission, direct the resources of the organization to achieve its defined goals, and make decisions that ensure the organization's effectiveness and continuity.

Defining objectives that guide sales-force activities to achieving desired sales-force behavior is a critical part of managing motivation. Some sales executives define their objectives along dimensions similar to the following:

☐ Beat last year's figures.

☐ Make budget.

☐ Sell more widgets.

☐ Open more new accounts.

☐ Get rid of the dead wood (accounts and/or sales reps).

☐ Reduce turnover.

Although these responses are reasonable and realistic, they evidence a short-run orientation. Moreover, attaching specific numbers to these objectives seldom provides sales reps and their managers with much in the way of direction (what to do). Indeed, for too many sales reps and field managers, quantitative objectives are threatening ("Make the numbers and you keep your job"), meaningless (see Potential in Part II), or childish (see Quotas in Part II). Perhaps the greatest danger in overemphasizing short-run, quantitative objectives is that they are self-limiting. Too many times, we only get what we ask for.

Many sales executives in high-performance sales organizations state their objectives more along the following lines:

☐ Organize and deploy our people to take better advantage of shifts in the competitive environment.

☐ Make better use of our human resources people to help us improve our hiring and promotion criteria.

☐ Find ways to improve the quantity and quality of our managers' time in the field.

☐ Design ways to provide more recognition to the deserving people and ways to encourage the poor performers to pursue their careers elsewhere.

☐ Assign clear responsibility to individuals to get the short-term objectives met and provide them with the resources they are going to need. Timetable: As close to yesterday as possible.

These kinds of objectives are challenging, meaningful, and rife with opportunities for creative solutions. None of them has boundaries, floors, or ceilings. As a consequence, the executives who set these goals are likely to get more than they ask for.

High-performance sales forces have clearly defined objectives that guide the behavior of their members in ways that serve the long-term interests of both the organization and its members. These sales executives avoid fuzzy abstractions like "increase sales" or "serve the customer," which allow people to do anything they interpret as being desirable. The better objectives are clear, concrete, realistic statements that focus attention on the performance of tasks relevant to achieving business-unit goals. Thus, "increase sales" might become "find, develop, and convert advanced high-technology processes into products and services that solve critical problems for potential customers in the worldwide forestry industry."

Clear objectives help keep your managers and sales reps from pursuing short-term advantages at the cost of achieving long-term goals. They help prevent sidetracking scarce resources to unsuitable and unproductive projects. They also help gain the commitment of managers and sales reps to tasks and projects by providing opportunities for them to see a clear and valuable relationship between the achievement of their own goals and the goals of the organization. Clear objectives help identify for the sales force those key activities and skills that build its distinctive competence—the ability to do well a particular kind of work that helps guarantee the organization's continuity. Clear objectives are a vital element in managing motivation.

NEWTON'S LAWS

IV. If you don't know where you're going,
any road will take you there.

Chapter 6

Tactical Decisions

Whereas strategic decisions are designed to ensure that the business unit is doing the right thing, tactical decisions are designed to ensure that the business unit is doing the thing right. Your managers should be as familiar with the reasoning behind the business unit's tactical activities as they are with its strategic activities. The choice of marketing tactics in particular has a heavy influence on the selling task.

Business-unit executives must decide whether to emphasize tactics that stimulate demand through aggressive vendor activity, known as push, or through aggressive appeals directly to consumers, known as pull. Push marketing motivates channels of distribution so that they in turn will motivate prospective customers to buy from them. Typical push tactics include aggressive personal selling, high dealer margins that encourage the channels to stock and to promote the product, protected trade territories that make it worthwhile for dealers to invest their time and efforts in selling the products, and attractive factory-service offerings and point-of-sale promotional efforts to help dealers sell the product.

Typical pull tactics include aggressive consumer advertising to stimulate consumers' interest, and broad distribution to ensure that consumers will find the product once they decide they want it. Pull tactics are usually correlated with limited manufacturers' service offerings and with low-dealer margins, because minimal dealer-selling activity is required.

Most marketing activity is a hybrid of push and pull tactics. Advertising aimed directly at the consumer can help the sales force; at the same time, an effective sales force can ensure that a nationally advertised product is stocked and promoted by retailers. Developing marketing tactics is a delicate balancing act. The firm's products must be matched to its potential customers. Advertising, pricing, distribution, and product policies must be coordinated with one another and with the various stages in each product's life cycle. Finally, product offerings must ensure that the financial needs of new products will be satisfied by funds generated by older products, while consumers' boredom with older products is compensated for by the interest stirred by the newer models.

In high-performance organizations, strategic decisions are made and broad tactical activities are defined by senior executives, including sales executives. The sales force is assigned the responsibility of implementing those strategic decisions and performing those tactical activities.

In the worst-case scenario—an all-too-frequent occurrence in low-performance sales forces—sales executives micro-manage the tactics (reviewing call reports is a good example) and sales reps make strategic decisions. An example of this scenario follows:

> Executives for a high-end furniture manufacturer decided to broaden distribution by selling certain of its lines through quality home centers. One sales rep with an outstanding performance record with "traditional" outlets and a large and prestigious territory was able to thwart this strategy by claiming "my current customers would reduce their orders if they knew I was selling to discounters."

An understanding of and a commitment to the business unit's strategy and the reasoning behind the tactical activities make up the "big picture." In high-performance sales forces, everyone from the sales and marketing executives to the sales reps shares a view of the same big picture. Managing motivation requires it.

Marketing strategy and tactics vary from competitor to competitor. As a consequence, sales tasks vary from competitor to competitor. It is useful for your field managers and sales reps to see how the selling tasks among even direct competitors can vary. This realization can help them understand the relationship between their activities on a day-to-day basis and the business unit's strategic and tactical objectives.

Leaving aside retail (over-the-counter) and delivery (filling inventory) selling, personal-selling activities fall into four tactical or task categories. Most firms use more than one selling tactic, but even in these hybrid situations, one category usually predominates. The attributes and skills required to carry out the four main selling tasks vary considerably. The managerial policies and procedures and the amounts and kinds of supervision appropriate to each tactical approach also differ.

TRADE SELLING

The primary responsibility of the trade-sales force is to build sales volume by providing the firm's customers with promotional assistance, thereby making the firm's resellers more effective. The trade-sales force therefore sells *through* rather than sells *to* its customers. Trade selling is common in many industries, but it predominates in consumer durables and nondurables such as furniture, apparel, textiles, and food, as well as in wholesaling firms. Because consumer products tend to be mature and are promoted directly to the user, a consumer-products firm's trade selling is often less critical to marketing success than are its advertising and promotion activities.

Nevertheless, if professional trade-sales reps are to help distributors and retailers, they must thoroughly understand how the customers run their businesses. Aggressiveness is probably less important than maturity, and technical competence is probably less important than "wearing well" with customers.

MISSIONARY SELLING

The missionary-sales force builds sales volume by persuading second-order or indirect customers to order from the firm's direct customers, which are its wholesalers and other channels of distribution. Thus, the missionary-sales force sells *for* its direct customers, whereas the trade-sales force sells through them. Missionary selling is common in the chemical, transportation, wholesaling, and pharmaceutical industries.

Whereas professional missionary-sales reps may not need to be particularly aggressive, good coverage of the market, efficiency in sales calls, and the ability to make a succinct yet persuasive presentation of product benefits are perhaps their most important skills.

TECHNICAL SELLING

The primary responsibility of the technical-sales force is to increase sales volume by providing the firm's customers with technical advice and assistance. Unlike the trade- or missionary-sales representative, the technical-sales rep sells directly *to* the user or buyer. Technical selling is common in the chemical, machinery, office products, and heavy-machinery industries.

Technical-sales reps—compared with the trade- or missionary-sales reps—are more likely to need consulting and analytical skills to enable them to identify and solve customers' problems. Technical-sales reps must also, however, have the interpersonal skills required for the other selling tasks. They must be able to persuade customers that the products can solve their problems. In requiring both sorts of skills, technical-sales reps resemble management consultants.

ENTREPRENEURIAL SELLING

The primary responsibility of the entrepreneurial-sales force is to obtain new accounts for its business unit. Converting a total stranger into a customer is the critical task. This kind of selling is variously called canvassing, bird dogging, and cold calling. Similar to technical selling, it is selling *to* customers. Unlike technical selling, entrepreneurial selling may require a great deal of aggressiveness and the capacity to withstand feelings of rejection when customers say no. Entrepreneurial selling is common in almost all industries.

Entrepreneurial-sales reps need to be aggressive self starters who can balance the all-too-infrequent exhilaration of making the sale with the all-too-frequent deflation that comes with polite—or sometimes brutal—rejection.

HYBRID SALES FORCES

To some extent, almost every sales organization is a hybrid of two or more of these four types of sales forces. Many sales jobs require new-business development in addition to trade, missionary, or technical selling. Many sales jobs require missionary work in addition to trade or technical selling.

Your managers must recognize that no two selling jobs are alike, even in firms competing in the same industry. Each firm will have a different marketing strategy, each strategy requiring different behavior from the sales force. It is important, therefore, that all parties involved—sales rep, field manager, sales executive, and marketing executive—understand in detail the desired sales-force behavior. The sales rep can then do the selling job as it should be done; the field manager can appropriately direct and coach the sales force; the sales executive can formulate policies and procedures to encourage the sales rep to do the job, and participate with the marketing executives to design marketing strategies that maximize the efficiency and effectiveness of the sales force.

NEWTON'S LAWS

V. Companies don't do things. People do.

Chapter 7

Commitment

Leadership is the management of motivation. Executives in high-performance organizations—sales and otherwise—view motivation as a concept that goes far beyond carrots and sticks, promotions and probations, cash and quotas. They view motivation as a collection of activities, values, and conditions that permeate the organization from the highest levels of decision making to the lowest. They view leadership, the management of motivation, as their most important responsibility.

All organizations need primary clienteles. In order to remain viable, organizations must create and maintain those clienteles. Political organizations must have constituents. Educational organizations must have students. Social organizations must have members. Business organizations must have customers.

Managing motivation in a business unit begins with a decision to compete for the creation and maintenance of customers in a particular way. This decision is the basis for your business unit's mission. It is a commitment to provide your current and potential customers with the goods and services they want. It is a commitment to provide the members of your business unit with a sense of where they are going and how they are going to get there. Without a sense of mission, your other motivational activities won't be optimized.

To be effective, your business unit's mission must satisfy at least three criteria. First, it must be reality-based, taking into consideration the present and potential threats and opportunities in your competitive environment and the present and potential strengths and limitations of your internal resources. Second, it must define creative goals that challenge the members of your business unit and reward them for outstanding performance. Third, it must identify and develop the business unit's distinctive competence, its ability to do well a particular kind of work.

For example, a division within a large health-care corporation describes its mission as designing, manufacturing, and marketing medical devices to aid in the treatment of emergency-health problems. Its goals include developing products that apply leading-edge technologies to the outpatient cardiac-care segment of the emergency-health-care market. Its distinctive competence is in the research and development of miniaturized electronic-transmission equipment. Its strategies are derived from these statements.

Managing motivation in a business unit includes formulating strategies to support its mission. Strategy is the pattern of objectives, major plans, and policies stated in such a way as to define the future course and character of the business unit. For many, if not most, business units, marketing strategy is the most important of its substrategies, because the primary responsibility of the marketing function is the creation and maintenance of a customer base. This same division defines its strategic objective as positioning itself with medical practitioners as the most reliable and reasonably priced supplier of cardiac-monitoring equipment. Its major plans and policies include heavy expenditures on R&D, penetration pricing on new products, and direct selling to selected cardiologists in major hospitals and university medical centers. The division finances its penetration-pricing strategy, large investments in R&D, and highly professional sales force by underinvesting in its stable of mature products.

When business-unit marketing strategy is effective, the sales organization grows in competence. Market segments are better identified, which leads to more efficient deployment of the sales force. Products and services are better designed, which leads to greater customer loyalty and more profitable repeat business. Appeals are better developed, which supports the sales reps with more effective advertising and promotion campaigns.

When marketing strategy is effective, the sales organization also grows in confidence. Evidence that your customers value your products and services and value the ability of your sales reps to help them solve their problems stimulates sales reps to accept greater challenges and take on more responsibility. Because sales reps find themselves performing well, they derive more satisfaction from their work.

In addition to defining the business unit's mission and formulating its strategy, managing motivation involves gaining the commitment of the business unit's members to its mission and its strategy. Gaining commitment involves infusing everyone with a sense of purpose and making everyone feel that their activities contribute to something important. Business-unit members begin to identify with the business unit, its subunits, and teams in ways that enhance their own self-esteem. They begin to view their leaders and managers as people whose ideas have economic and psychic value for them. They begin to become attached to their work as people doing things worthy of themselves instead of as workers merely earning a living. One sales rep in that division says, "To me, my job isn't selling. My job is keeping people alive and functioning well."

Leadership involves mission, strategy, commitment, and more. Part II of this book discusses the determination of policies and procedures that gain spontaneous and reasoned support for your business unit's mission and that facilitate the implementation of your business-unit and sales-force strategy.

PART II

THE SYSTEM: POLICIES AND PROCEDURES

Chapter 8

Policies

Most organizations have rules and regulations designed to encourage or discourage certain kinds of behavior among their members. Some of these rules and regulations are implicit—ways of saying and doing things that are never codified, just passed down from generation to generation—for example: what clothing and hair styles are appropriate for work, whether senior executives are called by their first names, how much confrontation is tolerated/expected/rewarded at meetings, what offices and other workspaces look like, whether alcohol is served at organizational functions, whether certain leisure activities (such as sports) are more acceptable than others, and whether spouses and/or significant others are invited to social functions.

Other rules and regulations are explicit and have been codified in some sort of "policy manual." In some organizations, the policy manual sits on a shelf and collects dust. In others, the policy manual is consulted before each and every decision is made. Whether referred to or not, the policy manual usually contains a description of the reporting relationships within the organization; how the workplace tasks are allocated and deployed; how people are recruited, selected, hired, and (ex)terminated; how performance is

monitored and appraised; how compensation and other work benefits are defined and administered; and what "rights" and "duties"
are conferred on "employer" and "employee" (and relevant grievance procedures).

Whether implicit or explicit, organization rules and regulations—
for purposes of simplification, I will call them "policies"—are the
organization's super ego—the collection of shoulds, musts, oughts,
and have-tos that let everybody know what acceptable behavior is.
Policy seldom defines what outstanding behavior is, however, or
what marginal or unacceptable behavior is. Those judgments are
left to the people who get paid to implement the policy. Some managers tend to go by the book. Such close adherence to the written
policies makes life easier, and it more or less guarantees "acceptable" behavior. Other managers try to understand how policies influence people's behavior. They try to comprehend both the letter
and the spirit of the law. They try to understand how policy is
determined and use that understanding to bring out the best in the
people around them.

In high-performance sales organizations, policies are designed to
facilitate the implementation of marketing strategy. Reporting relationships (often codified into "organization charts") are defined to
ensure responsibility, accountability, and efficiency in decision-
making activities, as well as to recognize and reward individual
competence. Policies are also established to maintain the proper
locus of decisions; that is, to make sure that the senior executives
responsible for making strategic decisions aren't preoccupied with
making tactical decisions and that the supervisory people responsible for making day-to-day operating decisions aren't unknowingly
making decisions that influence the future course and character of
the organization.

Closely related to the design of reporting relationships are policies
regarding the allocation of resources to the work that the organizations does; how the tasks are defined, staffed, and deployed; how
the performance of those tasks is monitored, appraised, and rewarded; and how the inevitable internal conflicts among people are
resolved.

THE MANAGEMENT SYSTEM

These kinds of policies, and others that guide, direct, and motivate the organization's members to pursue its strategic objectives are often referred to as the organization's *structure* or *management system*. I prefer the latter term because it connotes more a dynamic, changing, living, phenomenon than an inflexible structure.

In low-performance sales organizations, structures are "in place" because change is a phenomenon to be resisted. Executives and managers are involved (most of the time, desperately) in managing the status quo. These organizations are bureaucracies. In the same way that low-performance organizations change their strategies (usually because they have no choice), they also change their management systems. These changes are seldom rational responses to organizational realities; that is, getting it done. System changes in low-performance organizations are usually the consequence of the search for "Magic Bananas," described later in this discussion.

In high-performance sales organizations, the management system, as with the strategy, is under continuous review. Systems are always in flux, because the environment is always in flux. You should take pains to ensure not only the continuing viability of your business unit's strategy but also the current utility and relevance of your business unit's management system in encouraging desired behavior. Executives and managers are involved in managing change because that's what formulating and implementing organizational strategy is all about. Managing change is an activity central to managing motivation.

In high-performance sales organizations, system decisions receive the kind of constant attention that strategic decisions receive. Thus, as the sales organization undertakes new ventures, sales executives raise questions that begin the work of answering such questions as the following:

☐ What new skills, facilities, ideas, relationships, materials, finances, people, and technologies will be required?

☐ How should these new resources be fitted into the existing sales organization such that the whole will be greater than the sum of the parts?

☐ What potential shortfalls, roadblocks, and attitudes can arise to impede the sales organization's strivings, and how can these impediments be overcome?

As a sales executive in a high-performance organization, it's your job to produce answers to these questions and keep your field managers apprised of the reasons for the changes.

It's usually a lot easier to recognize and respond effectively to environmental events at the strategic level than to implement the required responses at the system level. But making sure that system decisions support strategic decisions can be a tricky business. Executives can decide to serve new markets, create new products, and satisfy new constituencies more quickly and easily than they can create system modifications (for example, compensation plans) to implement those decisions.

Experienced sales executives, therefore, are cautious about accepting advice from outsiders on how to design a system, or how to change one. What competitors do, what prestigious firms do, and what articles in learned journals suggest may not be relevant to the performance of your business unit's particular sales task. What may be good practice for one sales force may be wrong for another. Thus, in a high-performance sales force, executives continually ask themselves such questions as these:

☐ Are the sales reps deployed correctly?

☐ Are selection and training procedures effective?

☐ Are controls sufficient?

☐ Are sales reps being paid too little or too much?

☐ Are they adequately supervised?

☐ In short, are management policies and practices appropriate to the selling task as we define it today—not just "what we've always done"?

Strategic changes *always* produce changes in the selling task. Usually these changes are gradual and thus frequently are not clearly communicated to line managers or sales reps. If the sales-management system is not reviewed and kept in line with current desired behavior, executives may discover, belatedly, that strategy dictates one kind of behavior, whereas compensation, performance appraisal, and other policies encourage a different, and perhaps undesired, kind of behavior.

Of course, the sales-management system will not constitute all the influences on sales-force behavior. Common sense suggests that *how well* sales executives and their managers implement policies may have a greater impact on performance than *what* policies those executives choose to implement. Moreover, choice of the elements of the sales-management system are often influenced by outside factors such as industry norms or particular competitive situations.

MYTHOLOGY

Nevertheless, sales executives are responsible for deciding the most appropriate form of organization for their sales forces, the most appropriate selection criteria, compensation plan, span of control, and so forth. The major obstacle to thinking clearly about these decisions is mythology. Webster defines *myth* as "an ill-founded belief held uncritically, especially by an interested group." Although sales-management myths are legion, here are some common ones:

"Sales reps work harder for straight commission."

"College graduates are not interested in selling."

"Sales reps are born, not made."

Any one of these conclusions may have validity in the context of the particular situation within which it originated. But the theorems do not necessarily remain valid when they are applied to other, quite different situations. The point is that "best practice" needs to be highly particularized, and particularized right down to the individual business unit. Mythology is no substitute for a good, hard, close look at reality.

SYSTEM DECISIONS

Given a clear understanding of the business unit's marketing strategy and expectations regarding the behavior of its sales force, you can manage motivation better by choosing a judicious *combination* of policies and practices. To choose these policies and practices, you should consider the following factors:

☐ the organizational approach that best encourages the kind of sales-force behavior for which the marketing strategy calls

☐ the territory assignments that provide the best strategic support; that is, the most efficient and effective market coverage

☐ the kind of person best suited to the selling task

☐ the amount and kind of initial and subsequent training that best prepare sales reps to fulfill their role in the marketing strategy

☐ the level and method of compensation that best reward sales reps for performing their required tasks well

☐ the measures and controls that best serve to direct and monitor the desired sales-force behavior

☐ the system for evaluating sales-force performance that best encourages the desired performance

The *combination* of policies is what's important. To rely too heavily on one element of the sales-management system is to depend on mythology. For example, high-performance sales executives avoid placing a disproportionate emphasis on compensation plans. In effect, these sales executives have overcome the notion that "I can rely on my pay plan to get better performance." Most high-performance sales executives agree that compensation will influence sales-force behavior, but so will selection and training decisions. Sales executives who accept the fact that all of these decisions are highly interrelated recognize that the proper combination of policies and practices, each designed to encourage desired behavior, produces a total effect greater than the sum of the parts. It is this total effect you should seek in your efforts to manage motivation, not a Magic Banana.

MAGIC BANANAS

A *Magic Banana* is an organizational policy or procedure designed to get the gorillas (sales reps) to march steadfastly in rhythmic single file in pursuit of *the* banana (something you hope will produce better sales results). Examples of Magic Bananas are numerous:

"I was talking to a guy who works for General Bedlam. They organize their sales force into (fill in the blank). I'll bet we'll get better productivity from our sales reps if we organize them the same way. Let's reorganize!"

"I just finished reading this great book on motivation. Let's get the author in here to shape up our sales reps."

"We need smarter people around here. Tell our human resources people to start hiring some MBAs."

"We need more harmony around here. Tell our human resources people to start firing some MBAs."

"Let's send all our people to Swami Pajama's retreat and build some human-relations skills around here."

"Let's put a PC in everybody's office and see whether that doesn't improve the quality of our decisions."

"Our salespeople aren't selling enough. Let's change the compensation plan. What if we paid them 2 percent of the first three carloads, 3 percent on the next six, divide that by the percent increase in the gross national product, and . . ."

"Our people aren't working hard enough. We need a new performance-appraisal program (PAP). Let's get Entropy Associates in here to design one for us."

"Maybe if we just redesigned our stationery . . ."

Magic Bananas may smell good, but they seldom taste good. Because they tend to be fads or quick fixes, they tend to produce indigestion or leave a bad aftertaste. Nevertheless, some executives love Magic Bananas. They never stop looking for them. Magic Bananas represent the ultimate solution—the Big Fix. Smart managers should ignore Magic Bananas; the Big Fix won't work. Magic Bananas are no substitute for effective motivation management.

NEWTON'S LAWS

VI. There ain't no Magic Bananas;
at least, none that work.

Chapter 9

Organization

What type of sales-force organization suits your products and target markets? Should your organization be structured from the standpoint of the customer, the product line, or the geography of the market? Put another way, what type of organization best encourages the kind of behavior you want from your sales force?

When specialized knowledge of customer businesses is an essential sales force skill, sales forces are best organized by customer groups. For instance, many computer manufacturers assign one group of sales reps to call on retailers, another to call on banks, another to call on utilities, and so on. Each of these customer groups has different computer requirements. The training required to understand each business well enough to sell computer hardware and software to it is sufficiently different for each customer group to warrant separate sales groups.

When the product lines are sufficiently complex to warrant product specialists, sales forces are best organized by product line. For instance, many manufacturers of medical equipment assign one group of sales reps to sell kidney-dialysis equipment, another to sell X-ray equipment, another to sell surgical equipment, and so on.

Organization by geographical boundaries is best when customers are fairly homogeneous in their need for the product, when the product line is homogeneous or nontechnical, or when travel between accounts precludes efficient use of customer or product-line specialists.

Your sales managers should be led to expect periodic reorganization. As your markets, products, and customers change in response to changes in the competitive arena, your business unit must remain responsive. Don't overdo it, however, because reorganization can become a favorite Magic Banana, leaving everyone in a state of permanent instability.

DEPLOYMENT

When everything is going along well, routine attention to territory assignment will keep deployment issues from becoming a headache. When everything is not going along well or your business unit is experiencing a lot of strategic changes, deployment issues can become a migraine of severe proportions.

When things aren't going well, deployment issues become a headache because they are not recognized as a problem. The blame tends to fall on scapegoats such as specific people, the compensation plan, or the factory. In many instances, the real culprit is poor territory alignment. It creates inequitable workloads, unfair earning opportunities, customer dissatisfaction, and therefore low salesforce morale.

Deployment issues can also become a headache because strategic change always produces task change. And a significant part of task change involves a reassessment of who goes where, and with what frequency, to say and do what to whom. The more significant the strategic change, the more significant the task change. Except for your Eagles, everyone will resist change, so the human-relations issues will be as complex as the deployment decisions.

In making deployment decisions (usually manifested in territory realignment), most sales executives try to balance territory workload, territory potential, territory sales volume, and sales reps' and customer characteristics. A full day's work is usually the prerequisite. Before designing territories that fit this simple criterion, however, you have to consider such complicating factors as minimum account size for profitability, optimal call frequency for maintaining or converting customers, and optimal sales-force size. Two common formulas that aid in making these calculations are:

$$\frac{\text{Required maintenance and conversion time per account}}{\text{Available selling time per sales rep}} \times \text{No. of accounts} = \text{No. of sales reps}$$

$$\frac{\text{Acceptable sales expense}}{\text{Average cost per sales rep}} = \text{No. of sales reps}$$

For more complex situations (most are), computer programs are available that draw maps of sales territories. These programs enable you to manipulate a number of variables simultaneously, such as required time for each account, hours available, travel distances, and geographic contiguity. Furthermore, linear-programming models are available to help you make decisions regarding minimum account profitability and the balance between spending time on converting or maintaining accounts. All these formulas and programs can help, but even when territories are assigned to perfection, there is no guarantee that sales reps will perform to the limit of their capabilities. (Nor will customers behave as the models predict.) Nevertheless, when territories are badly aligned, sales will always suffer.

POTENTIAL

Territories with unequal potential provide you with opportunities to make some territories "better" than others in order to match your Eagles with your best customers, allow for promotions within grade, create training territories, or take advantage of individual selling personalities (for example, "country boys").

Territories with equal potential theoretically give sales reps equal earning opportunities and provide sales managers with opportunities to make performance comparisons. Keep in mind, however, that sales territories are really "black boxes." The sales rep's skill and effort go in at one end. Sales results come out the other. Within the black box the territory variables come into play: the quality and intensity of competition; the degree of product saturation (the opportunity to make an initial or subsequent sale); the past history of customer relationships; travel requirements and other physical characteristics; and so on. Except in rare instances, territory variables defy precise quantitative analyses. As a consequence, experienced sales executives avoid jumping to conclusions regarding the relationship between a sales rep's skill and effort and his or her short-term sales results.

Many executives in high-performance sales organizations use the word potential with a great deal of caution when referring to future sales. So should your managers. What does potential mean? Where do the numbers come from?

The answer to the first question can range from "all the business out there" to "all the available business out there." It can be "everyone should have at least one of our widgets" or "everyone should have at least 30 of our widgets." Management suspicion of this term is well founded. Most sales reps are even more suspicious. The difference between "all business" and "available business" is meaningful to anyone who has ever faced entrenched competition. Furthermore, the definition of "available business" is subject to a great deal of interpretation on the part of the people concerned. Seldom do managers and sales reps agree; so why introduce another source of useless friction?

The answer to the second question is even more fraught with conflict. Seldom is a sales organization fortunate enough to have access to numbers that reflect reality when it comes to estimating potential. Too often "potential" is established by staff personnel who wouldn't recognize a customer if they ran over one in the parking lot. The problem is really compounded when your sales operation is global.

Measures of potential have one important function, however. They permit comparisons of performance among territories and sales reps and help align territories when roughly equivalent sales opportunities are important. Under these circumstances, it is less important for potential to be exact than for the number to be fair and applied evenhandedly across the board. Many high-performance sales organizations rely on outside sources to calculate a given territory's share of expected business. The managers take it from there by adjusting for known competitive conditions and use these data to compare the sales performance in one territory with another. In many instances, these data are not shared with sales reps; evaluating is done on a personal basis without reference to these kinds of numbers, which can cause rancor and lethargy.

CALL REPORTS

Many high-performance sales forces don't use call reports. As with other forms of paperwork, filling them out takes time away from selling. Reviewing them takes time away from field supervision. Following through on them in any positive way is such a rare occurrence that many firms view a call-report system as a waste of time and money. A common view held by many executives is that you either trust your sales reps to know what they are doing or you don't; you either assume your sales reps are working hard or you don't. Either way, submitting call reports won't help.

If you must use call reports (and many high-performance sales forces do), employ them to gather useful information. And make sure the information is more useful to the sales rep than it is to you; otherwise, garbage in, garbage out.

Two kinds of useful information are marketing intelligence and deployment data. Many executives find it useful to separate these data by information channel. Marketing intelligence (for example, observations about competitive activities or customer reactions) can be communicated by sales reps directly to product managers or staff personnel through devices such as voice mail. The office personnel collate the data and inform the parties responsible for strategic or tactical action. This method is easy for the sales reps. They don't have to write essays. It's efficient for the business unit. The people who need the information get it quickly. It only works well, however, when the people who get the information personally thank the sales reps for giving it to them.

Collecting useful deployment data requires an analysis of what you need to know and a decision as to who best can collect it. A lot of information commonly needed for reports can be easily obtained from invoices. Facts about who the sales rep is calling on or not calling on, however, cannot be obtained this way.

Before you try to collect deployment information you need to know why you are collecting it. If it is to check up on your sales reps, replace them now and hire some people you can trust. If it is to help your sales reps deploy themselves better, they need more information about the calls they made than simply the names of the people they called on. They need to know whether they are spending their time wisely.

Time in the day is the one gift that everyone has in equal measure. How people spend their time distinguishes them from one another. In a very real sense, then, an important part of your field sales managers' job is to help your sales reps maximize their use of every working minute. What your Eagles would really like to know is how they spend their time relative to the highest flyers. For instance, how much time do they spend on these tasks:

	By Customer	By Prospect
Traveling		
Gathering data		
Making presentations		
Solving problems		
Closing deals		

and on:

Office paperwork

Personal call planning

Internal liaison

Other miscellaneous

Gathering these kinds of data, organizing them in a time study, and disseminating them *uncritically* enables sales reps to see how they spend their time in comparison with the average and best performers, and to work toward (or seek help in) reallocating their time accordingly.

This kind of information is also useful to you and your managers. It permits you to make better decisions regarding manpower needs, territory design, and training and supervisory activities.

It takes a highly sophisticated management team and a lot of mutual trust to make an information system like this one work. Because a successful sales-management information system depends on the sales reps to supply the data bank, no sales rep should be punished in any way for supplying any kind of information. The system collapses instantly with the first "What were you doing on Wednesday afternoon?" The temptation to ask such questions is strong, however, which is why so few organizations use a time-study approach.

If you want to try using such a system, make sure that: (1) your management philosophy is to *help* sales reps sell, not to *force* them to sell; (2) your management approach is more concerned with monitoring business-unit performance than with individual performance; (3) your management policies complement and encourage communications flow rather than inhibit or distort it; and (4) your managers' styles engender rather than inhibit cooperation.

A rather tall order.

QUOTAS

Your field managers must communicate sales objectives to their sales reps. Many business units use personal sales quotas to make these objectives clear. Some companies view quotas as forecasts: They expect quotas to be met. Other companies view quotas as targets: they expect only the best sales reps to meet them. Other companies view quotas as the margin: Make them and you get to keep your job. Still other companies use quotas as a basis for compensation.

To administer quotas effectively, your managers must understand their purpose and understand the influence that they exert on sales reps in various situations. Some companies base quotas, a word from Latin meaning "shares," on historical sales performance; others on estimates of sales potential; still others attempt to tailor the quotas to the strengths and weaknesses of the individual sales reps.

Quotas based on historical sales (often called ratchets when they are based on percentage increases over the previous year's sales) tend to give the better sales reps the harder challenge, as they must get more and more sales from the same territory. Quotas based on potential sales tend to give the weaker sales reps the harder challenge, for the potential in their territories grows faster than their abilities. Quotas personalized to challenge strong and weak performers equally provide neither the ability to forecast sales that historical quotas do, nor the ability to make comparative evaluations that quotas based on potential do.

Executives in many high-performance sales forces avoid the use of quotas altogether, because quotas can give an impression of precision where none exists. In addition, such quotas can appear arbitrary to sales reps, and a serious threat to morale if their compensation is tied to these arbitrary numbers. Those who avoid quotas believe that mature, responsible people, given an opportunity to do their best, will indeed do their best, and that arbitrary quotas are, therefore, not only superfluous but childish.

An alternative to quotas based on historical or potential measures is the personal quota: the *correct* application of management by objectives (MBO). Most MBO systems fail for two reasons. First, sales reps are encouraged to set objectives for themselves, but then senior managers don't buy the sales reps' objectives. Once the objectives are changed (usually upwards!), the system collapses. Second, MBO contains no contract between sales rep and manager; that is, no joint sales-rep and manager commitment exists. The correct application of MBO involves *joint* goal setting and *joint* effort to achieve those goals. An example best illustrates the contractual nature of MBO:

> A sales rep and a manager jointly examine the performance of the 20 percent of the sales rep's accounts that produce 80 percent of her results. The sales rep suggests a target to shoot for. The manager suggests another target based on a specific commitment to help the sales rep meet the manager's target:

> Boss: If I commit to making three extra field visits with you on each of these four accounts we have identified as prospects for increased sales, will you commit to increasing their sales by 10 percent?

> Sally: With that amount of attention, I think we could do it. Yes, I'll commit.

> Boss: It's a deal. Remember, if I don't live up to my promise, you're not responsible for the percentage increase.

The involvement, teamwork, commitment, and challenge inherent in this kind of contractual application of MBO makes it a powerful influence on performance, and an important element in managing motivation.

NEWTON'S LAWS

VII. If you extrapolate too much, you'll go blind.

Chapter 10

Selection

In high-performance sales forces, hiring to fill territories and the frequent consequence—hiring less-than-outstanding candidates—are avoided at all costs. The common philosophy among these sales organizations is an insistence on hiring only potential Eagles. Put another way: Don't waste everyone's time trying to improve the behavior of people who will never become Eagles.

Selection criteria should weed out people who lack the skills—analytical, planning, organizing, interpersonal, and persuasive—for the business unit's selling task. In some sales jobs, one or more of these skills may not be necessary; in others, one or more may be critical. The search for generalized "sales aptitude" may lead to hiring the "all-around athlete" or someone who "seems to fit," a person who may look like the ideal sales rep but who lacks a key skill.

Selection criteria should also weed out people who lack the attributes for the business unit's selling task—product, customer, or industry familiarity; dependability; initiative; and creativity. Again, some of these attributes may not be necessary; others may be critical.

High-performance sales-force executives seek Eagles. They value diversity. But they seldom gamble. Eagles come in all colors, sizes, genders and backgrounds, so by seeking excellence without bias, in one stroke managers achieve diversity and avoid mediocrity. Many managers restrict their choices to people with high credentials in education (not necessarily formal education), experience, and proven track records, because leopards don't change their spots. Eagles don't change their markings, either. These high-performance sales executives prefer to cherry-pick the best from other sales organizations. Hiring excellent people virtually guarantees the opportunity to develop a high-performance sales force. It's not easy, however; Eagles don't flock. You have to find them one at a time.

PROMOTABILITY

In healthy organizations, people get promoted primarily because they are performing their current jobs in outstanding fashion. Consequently, many sales executives take the notion of promotability as a criterion for hiring with a grain of salt: It is difficult enough to make a hiring decision for an immediate job opening without compounding the situation by attempting to determine how that individual is going to perform on future jobs. Future jobs represent promotions, which are typically positions with different degrees of skill requirements and responsibility from the current positions. Someone's ability to advance in an organization is best evidenced by on-the-job performance and factors such as the ability and willingness to modify one's behavior to establish proper priorities and satisfy the demands of self, subordinates, bosses, business unit goals, and ethics.

Do the best sales reps make the best managers? Sometimes yes, sometimes no. A good gauge, however, is the degree of managerial content in the selling job. If the selling job is low in managerial content (that is, involves little relationship-building inside or outside the business unit; little planning, organizing, and analyzing skills; and requires little long-term perspective), your best sales reps are not likely to be strong managers. On the other hand, if the selling task has a heavy managerial content, an outstanding sales rep is likely to become an outstanding manager.

The lack of a system for counseling and encouraging gifted people to consider becoming managers, however, will make identifying and developing future managers difficult. Clear-cut management-development goals are as necessary in the long run as clear-cut performance goals are in the short-run. A big help in this area is to design career paths—beginning at the sales-rep level—that permit the development of skills that will lead to success at each subsequent level.

SELECTION METHODS

Sales executives must decide what kind of person is best suited to the business unit's selling task. Your decision involves determining the best sources of applicants for sales positions, the economics of poor performers and sales-force turnover, the desirability of psychological testing, and the role of personal judgment in selecting salespeople.

Mythology can hamper the process of making good selection decisions. As mentioned previously, experienced sales executives try to understand the particular requirements of the sales job, rather than seeking the "ideal sales type." Because managing motivation begins with hiring the best people, the steps outlined here are a good place to start.

Set Hiring Guidelines by the Realities of the Selling Task

What key activities need to be performed? How much supervision is available? What is the risk to the business unit if the sales rep fails to perform well? What are the travel requirements? How much liaison is required between sales reps and other company personnel? Answers to these and similar questions help you appraise the details of the sales job realistically and thereby avoid general criteria that provide few useful hiring guidelines.

Check for Minimal Prerequisites

Such things as experience, education, and other prerequisites, developed from an analysis of the realities of the job, can usually be inspected on an application form.

Check for Required Skills

Skills and aptitudes are often fairly easy to observe or measure. A good interviewer can evaluate a candidate's articulateness and, to a lesser degree, selling ability and analytical skills.

Check for the Personal Qualities Needed

Beyond minimum acceptable levels, personal qualities are usually hard to observe or measure. A good interviewer can evaluate a candidate's appearance and poise. Beyond these, however, identifying the degree of such qualities as judgment, maturity, motivation, character, and so forth, seem to defy both skilled interviewers and written tests (short of psychiatric diagnostic devices such as the Rorschach and Thematic Apperception Tests).

Determine Whether to Use More Complex Tests

The truly critical attributes—what you would really like to know about applicants—are unmeasurable. How will the customer react to them? Will they work hard? Are they dependable, honest? Will they show initiative? Are psychological tests the answer to these kinds of questions?

Determine Whether to Involve Staff Specialists

The obvious disadvantage is that first-line managers lose the opportunity to develop their judgment and be accountable for their actions. (Making a few hiring mistakes has the effect of making a manager much wiser much faster!) Should field sales managers, however, become involved in selection and hiring decisions? In many high-performance sales forces, the answer is "no." Field sales managers have the responsibility for on-the-job training, coaching, counseling, and evaluating the performance of their sales reps. These activities are usually a full-time job. Nevertheless, some executives view field sales management involvement in selection interviews as a training activity to prepare them for promotion. Here is how one high-performance sales force does it:

1. Applicants are recruited and screened by the folks in Human Resources.[1]

2. Applicants deemed suitable and desirable by the folks in Human Resources are interviewed by a regional sales manager in the presence of a district sales manager who reports to the regional sales manager. (The applicant may or may not be eventually assigned to this particular district sales manager.)

3. The district sales manager is free to participate in the interview. At the close of the interview (after the applicant has left), the regional sales manager asks the district sales manager whether the applicant should be hired. If the district sales manager says "no," the applicant is not hired. If the district sales manager says "yes," the regional sales manager can concur or overrule. In either case, the regional and district sales managers discuss at length the reasoning behind each other's thinking.

By the time the district sales manager assumes a regional sales manager's responsibilities, he or she has gained useful insights into (and practical experience assessing) the skills, aptitudes, and attitudes that make up the sales task's key success factors.

---

[1] A nauseating title for a critical function. What was wrong with *personnel?* If your organization really cared about people, would it call them *human resources?*

PSYCHOLOGICAL TESTING

Psychological testing can be a valuable tool in avoiding certain high-risk situations. It has its place—but seldom in sales-force selection procedures. The best candidates can usually be identified by applying management judgment to a careful analysis of the requirements of the job—the desired behavior.

In instances where key skills are involved (such as driving a truck or programming a computer), a simple test can weed out the incompetent. In instances where a "quick-and-dirty" screening is required to supplement the judgment of inexperienced field sales managers, simple intelligence or sales-aptitude tests are similarly effective at weeding out the incompetent. This latter instance, however, is seldom faced by the high-performance sales force, because selection procedures are too important to involve the field managers directly. Their time is spent training sales reps, not hiring them.

Using psychological tests, however, has five real drawbacks:

☐ Many of these tests have been developed for other purposes—measuring general intelligence, vocational interests, or personality disorders. Their relevance to your sales tasks is more academic than practical. Even so-called sales-aptitude tests have limited relevance. The selling task varies so much from company to company and industry to industry that sales aptitude becomes a useless generality. Even when tailored to a specific business unit's selling task the tests can lead to "cloning": an insidious condition that helps ensure that today's key success factors will be perpetuated into tomorrow's competitive environment. Cloning is a sure road to organization vitrification.

☐ Psychological tests rarely predict success on the job. In that sense, they are like college entrance exams: whereas very low SAT scores indicate trouble ahead, many students with marginal SAT scores make Phi Beta Kappa because college turns them on; many with high SAT scores drop out because college turns them off. Selling is the same. Because experienced interviewers can also predict failure, why bother with testing? In addition, many minorities and women have difficulty scoring well on tests that have been developed primarily by white males with advanced degrees. Thus, besides being discriminatory, many of these tests weed out the diverse, creative, and potentially outstanding Eagles you are looking for.

☐ Some firms keep selection-test results in an individual's personnel file for later use in making promotion decisions. These data often are presented in technical terms that are hard for laypeople to interpret. How many of your managers know the significance of the difference between 128 and 132 on an IQ test? These kinds of data can lead to promoting one person over another because one is "more intelligent."

☐ The most important reason to avoid psychological testing is that reliance on these kinds of data—and they do make a seductive crutch—precludes the development of your managers' skills in judging people's likely behavior. A few hiring mistakes won't kill an organization; a bunch of nonthinking managers will.

☐ I—and a lot of high-performance sales executives—believe that the dissemination of psychological test data is unethical unless the candidate is given the opportunity to censor the test results. A psychiatrist used to administer tests, as a physician, is bound by the Hippocratic oath not to reveal data without the candidate's (patient's) permission. Most testing is done by laypeople, however, or by psychologists with M.A. or Ph.D. degrees who are not bound to protect an individual's privacy.

NEWTON'S LAWS

VIII. Seek excellence without bias and you will acheive diversity and avoid mediocrity.

Chapter 11

Training

The training task is made easier when the most adaptable candidates—those best suited to perform the sales task well—are hired in the first place. Managers are not paid to "develop" people; they are paid to help them modify their work-related behavior to fit the demands of your sales task. Training is your field sales managers' most important (ideally, their sole) responsibility.

Training activities fall into three categories: initial, continuation, and field (on-the-job) training. *Initial training* should be of sufficient duration and thoroughness to close the gap between the skills and aptitudes that the candidates bring with them and the skills and aptitudes required to perform the selling task (desired behavior). High-performance sales forces usually provide specialists to perform initial training activities—people skilled in assessing candidates' strengths and weaknesses, thoroughly familiar with the realities of the selling task and working climate, and highly effective in imparting the industry, product, and selling knowledge required to get your Eagles off the ground.

Continuation (sometimes called *refresher*) *training* is critical if your marketing plans, product line, or sales tactics change. For most high-performance sales forces, one or more of these conditions is an annual event. For consistency of message and clarity of communication, many high-performance sales-force executives delegate continuation training to training specialists also.

Field training is the field sales manager's job. He or she is the centurion whose primary responsibility is to ensure that desired behavior conforms to actual behavior. To manage motivation well, your field sales managers must be given the time, resources, and support to do the field training job well. If your field sales managers don't understand the realities of the sales task as defined by your business unit's marketing strategy, you will have as many strategies as you have field sales managers. If your field sales managers don't spend time in the field monitoring and modifying the behavior of your sales reps, you will have as many strategies as you have sales reps.

80-20 RULE

If your business is like the vast majority of those out there, 80 percent of your profit comes from 20 percent of your customers, 80 percent of your sales revenue comes from 20 percent of your sales reps, and 80 percent of your results comes from 20 percent of your activities.

Some of your managers may not be aware of this universal truth. In the hope that, somehow, a low-potential account can be "developed," they assign it to one of their Eagles. Hope seldom triumphs over experience. Even Eagles can't sell everybody. Eighty percent of your customers can probably be better and much less expensively serviced through telemarketing.

In the hope that somehow a poor-performing sales rep can be "developed," some of your managers may be wasting their scarcest resource—time—on this fruitless endeavor. Even if your most talented managers can improve a sales rep's poor performance, they can't make an Eagle out of a turkey.

The only way to break the 80-20 rule is to attract, hire, and feed your Eagles so that your Eagles crowd the other birds out of your nest. Get your field managers to spend 80 percent of their time with their Eagles, and you're home free.

Your field sales managers, therefore, need training, too. Initial training should follow as soon as possible after their promotion (prepromotion management training has its advocates, but many firms find the "crown prince" syndrome too tricky to deal with). Continuation training should ensure that the managerial skill development keeps pace with the growing technical and interpersonal skill development required of the selling task. The on-the-job coaching and counseling are as important for field managers as they are for their sales reps.

NEWTON'S LAWS

IX. There is nothing more frightful
than ignorance in action.

Goethe

Chapter 12

Compensation

Compensation is no substitute for management. I have yet to see a good compensation plan. The best ones are those that get in your managers' way the least. The best compensation plans reward performance rather than try to stimulate it. This difference is subtle but important. The former view, reward for performance, suggests that compensation is but one element in a system of policies and procedures designed to encourage sales reps to perform well. A compensation plan doesn't stand alone. Hiring only Eagles, the effectiveness of training programs, the quality of field supervision, the presence of nonfinancial forms of recognition, and many other factors combine with the compensation plan to create a high-performance climate. The view that compensation plans stimulate performance can lead to overreliance on compensation to manage motivation, and overlooks the fact that sales reps may desire recognition, advancement, challenge, and camaraderie in their work as well as money.

The choice of the kinds of behavior that financial compensation is to reward can be a puzzling one. On the one hand, if you want to stress short-run goals—such as opening new accounts, pushing products with higher margins, unloading products about to be phased out, or attempting to meet time-period volume objectives—your compensation plan is likely to include highly specific and objective criteria. On the other hand, if you want to stress long-term market development, if you experience selling cycles (from initial contact to signed order) that are longer than normal accounting or performance-appraisal periods, or if the selling effort requires tasks that only indirectly produce a sale, as in some types of trade and missionary selling, your compensation plan should probably be based on more general and subjective criteria.

How much to pay sales reps is another puzzling choice. You need to strike a balance between an amount that will attract and retain Eagles and an amount that makes economic sense to your business unit. Paying too little generally promotes excessive turnover; paying too much neither improves performance nor lowers turnover.[2] Within the dilemma of how much to pay are questions of the size of the pay differentials among your sales reps and whether the differences should be based on performance, merit (if it differs from performance), or seniority. One approach to these issues is to ask yourself: What am I willing to pay for the lowest acceptable performance, for average performance, and for outstanding performance? A graph similar to that in Figure 3 can be constructed.

The X axis and the points a, b, and c are usually determined by the marketplace—industry norms, competitive factors, and the supply of and demand for labor. The Y axis and the points low, average,

FIGURE 3

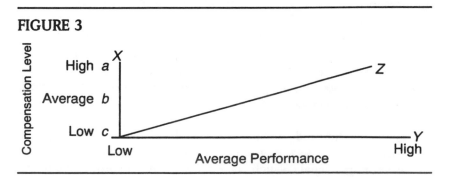

[2]See my monograph, *Sales Force Performance and Turnover* (Marketing Science Institute, 1973).

and high are usually determined from an economic analysis of your cost of selling. The slope and shape of the line Z is a function of the importance of personal selling in the marketing activity of the firm. If the sales reps' efforts are directly related to sales volume produced, it may be possible to reward them in a linear fashion, as the solid line in the graph indicates, because a high proportion of variable pay is warranted. This condition is most apt to be present when the selling cycle is short, sales reps are the dominant element in your marketing activity (the customer is created and maintained through the activities of the individual sales rep), and when the sales force shares little responsibility with other groups within the business unit for ensuring customer awareness of product benefits and satisfaction with product use. Examples of direct relationships between sales-force performance and sales volume produced can be found in many areas of entrepreneurial selling, such as the door-to-door selling of vacuum cleaners.

In most firms, relating sales-force performance directly to sales-volume produced is more difficult than in this first example. Many sales require a long time to consummate, are the result of teamwork with other internal departments, and involve a variety of activities that, when performed well, eventually produce both sales and long-term relationships with customers. To evaluate a sales rep's contributions to this kind of sales effort, some executives redefine performance as "merit," a term that covers numerous activities that indirectly produce sales volume. Here the attempt is to evaluate sales reps according to their performance of these activities and compensate them accordingly, while recognizing the dangers of subjectivity inherent in these evaluations. The nature of indirect selling, and the subjective element in appraising its performance, suggests that variable pay for this type of selling will be a smaller proportion of the sales rep's compensation than for direct selling. When neither sales volume nor merit is easy to assess, some executives rely on seniority to make distinctions among pay levels. Here the pay plans contain little if any variable element.

The format of the compensation plan can be important to both the sales force and the business unit. Even a carefully designed compensation plan can overpay for unintended results, as in the case of windfall sales; can underpay, as in the case of insufficient goods available from the factory; or can reward the wrong kind of behavior, as in the case of rewarding short-term sales at the expense of long-term relationships. The best compensation plans are those that are easy for you to administer; readily understandable and perceived by the sales reps as fair; flexible enough to withstand windfalls and catastrophes; and related to the sales rep's performance, whether that be sales volume or merit. In other words, the rewards should be seen as going to the deserving.

A good way to compensate your field sales managers is to tie their compensation to the compensation of the people they are paid to supervise. This policy leads to *goal congruence,* a situation in which your managers make more money when their coaching efforts and skill help their people become better sales reps and one in which your sales reps acknowledge that they make more money as a consequence of their field sales managers' coaching efforts and skill.

BONUS

Bonus usually implies a lump sum, paid periodically (usually annually) for the achievement of a specific target or targets, and awarded on either a group or individual basis.

From the Latin word meaning "good" (therefore, hard to argue with), bonuses nevertheless have their pitfalls:

☐ Bonuses should be a reward for specific performance, not a salary supplement. When viewed as the latter, they lose whatever power to reward they have and tend to alienate your high performers. When everyone gets a bonus, it denigrates the efforts of those who deserve the reward the most.

☐ The criteria for awarding bonuses should never be vague or abstract. Subjectivity invites favoritism.

☐ Neither should bonuses be based on the satisfactory performance of key activities; those are expected of everyone. To achieve maximum bang from your incentive buck, base your bonuses on performance above and beyond the call of duty.

Bonuses awarded on a group basis have their own additional pitfalls:

☐ Avoid group bonuses when the discrepancy between a group's best and worst performers is readily apparent. No one enjoys carrying dead wood.

☐ Avoid group bonuses when they tend to be automatic, as with those based on "corporate performance." After several "good" years, the impact of a "bad" year can be devastating to personal budgets and sales-force morale.

A bonus can be an important part of your total compensation plan, which in turn can be an important part of your total management system. Unless you're careful, however, a bonus can also be, as the Romans said, "malus."

COMMISSION

Commission is a form of compensation that pays sales reps a stated percentage or amount on each sale they make. Commission plans have a number of advantages:

☐ They reward results (sales made).

☐ They foster an entrepreneurial spirit: "The harder I work the more I make."

☐ If commissions are a substantial or total part of the compensation plan, they are a variable cost to the firm but a fixed and predictable cost per unit sold.

Commission plans also have disadvantages:

☐ Although the plans reward results, these results may tend to be short-term, and such a focus can potentially jeopardize long-term relationships. Sometimes the opportunity (or pressure) to sell something *now* results in a customer buying something not needed or wanted *ever*.

☐ Although commission plans foster an entrepreneurial spirit, that spirit may be hard to manage. Without managers and management systems to foster goal congruence, allowing sales reps to act solely in *their* best interests is unlikely to produce behavior that is in *your* best interest.

☐ When sales volume goes up, along with rising cost of goods sold and cost of doing business, commission plans can produce higher than usual expenses that erode profitability.

Variable expenses are acceptable when products are new and sales volume is uncertain. When products take off and profits roll in, however, give me fixed costs anytime. (Manufacturers' reps' financial lives are precarious for this very reason: If the products they represent get too successful in the marketplace, their clients begin to favor the fixed costs associated with having an in-house sales force.)

SALARY

A fixed amount paid on a regular basis, salaries are the base points for most compensation plans (with the exception of straight commission). Salaries combined with commission and/or bonus plans represent the majority of sales-force compensation systems. Straight-salary plans are less common but prevail in certain circumstances:

☐ *When relating the sales rep's efforts to specific sales results is difficult.* This situation is common in trade selling, where advertising or other forms of marketing activity are the dominant influences on customer behavior and the personal selling activity is restricted to the more mundane tasks of maintaining adequate inventory levels or setting up promotional displays.

☐ *When relating the sales rep's efforts to the behavior of specific purchasers is difficult.* This situation is common in missionary selling, where sales activities are directed toward "specifiers" such as doctors, and actual customer purchases are influenced by these third parties.

☐ *When the time required to consummate a sale is longer than the pay period.* This situation is common to "big ticket" items such as oil-drilling equipment, where a sale may take several years to consummate.

☐ *When isolating the impact of one person's activities on another's in the consummation of a sale is difficult.* This situation is common in team selling, where several business-unit nonsales personnel (such as product managers, engineers, financial analysts) contribute heavily to the consummation of the sale and the sales rep's function is to bring business-unit resources to bear on solving customer problems.

Many sales executives like straight-salary plans because sales costs are relatively fixed and sales activities are perceived as being tightly controlled. Other sales executives dislike straight-salary plans because they provide insufficient "motivation." Executives in high-performance sales organizations look for other, usually better, ways to "control" and "motivate" sales reps. Instead they manage motivation by basing their decisions about compensation plans on the nature of the selling task and the desired behavior of the sales reps.

One cautionary note about straight salary plans: high-performance organizations avoid awarding across-the-board (same percentage) raises to everyone; it denigrates the efforts of Eagles and stimulates lethargy on the part of marginal performers. Instead, try giving a big raise to the deserving—it's like a bonus—and no raise at all to the marginal. It sends out a strong message to people you are attempting to counsel out.

EXPENSE ACCOUNTS

Penny wise, pound foolish is the rule for expense accounts. On the other hand, expense accounts should *not* be part of the compensation plan. Clear guidelines really help avoid abuse. So does knowing when to make exceptions.

Reporting expenses is a necessary evil, and someone needs to keep track of where the money's going—but that someone is not the field sales manager. Checking expense reports is another of those activities in which field managers should not be engaged. It is a job best left to people in the accounting department; that's what they're paid for.

In disputes with the accounting department, make sure your managers side with their sales reps. If sales reps can't be trusted to account for sales expenses honestly and accurately, your managers should replace them.

FRINGE BENEFITS

Again, penny wise, pound foolish applies. Unlike expense accounts, however, fringe benefits *are* part of the compensation plan. An attractive fringe benefit package can be a powerful incentive to reduce turnover among your Eagles. It builds morale, invites loyalty, and lowers the stress that arises from the feelings of risk and ambiguity commonly associated with sales activities. Unfortunately, an attractive fringe-benefit package can be a powerful incentive to reduce turnover among low-performing sales reps, too. This situation should not militate against fringe benefits, however. Turnover among low-performing sales reps can be escalated by other means, such as counseling out (discussed in Part III) and publishing sales standings.

Good fringe benefits don't come cheap, but if they help you retain your Eagles, they are a worthwhile expense. Here are some ideas:

Hospitalization and Major Medical Insurance

Go for deluxe coverage. It alleviates a major concern for most people. Consider dental and legal insurance also.

Group Life Insurance

A little extra premium buys a lot more coverage. Don't be cheap, particularly if your Eagles are hatching a lot of eaglets.

Second-Mortgage and Education Loans

These opportunities are less common than other fringe benefits, which makes them all the more desirable. Arrange them through third parties on a shared-interest basis.

Maternity and Paternity Leave

Full-pay, six-month maternity and one-month paternity leaves are not unusual in non-English-speaking industrialized nations.

One-Month Paid Vacations

Why do English-speaking industrial concerns provide an annual vacation period of just two weeks? If you want your Eagles to live longer and enjoy productive lives, force them to take a month off every year.

"No-strings" Promotion Policy

If your employees are offered a promotion and they don't want it now (for example, if their child is in high school and they don't want to move), guarantee the offer until their circumstances change.

Ask the folks in Human Resources to cost these ideas out. Calculating on a per-Eagle basis, you'll be surprised at how low the benefits price tag is. After a few years of experience, you'll be surprised at how much return you get for the money spent.

NEWTON'S LAWS

X. Compensation is no substitute for management.

Chapter 13

Incentives

It's hard to argue with incentives. But sometimes they backfire. Then they become disincentives. Thoughtfully applied incentive practices encourage desired behavior. The following discussion describes the advantages and caveat's of commonly used incentive practices as seen by sales executives who are experts in managing motivation.

NEWSLETTERS

A sales rep's life can be a lonely one. Much of his or her time is spent traveling alone; waiting to see customers; calling on perfect strangers; and in general taking the brunt of whatever complaints all and sundry have regarding the organization, the product line, the service, billing procedures, credit terms, pricing policies, and so on. Of course, many of the sales rep's rewards come from these same encounters: Many derive great personal satisfaction from business relationships developed with people outside the firm.

Nevertheless, many of your sales reps (particularly those with high needs for affiliation) derive equal, if not greater, personal satisfaction from being an important member of a team. This team feeling is particularly important but difficult to instill within large sales forces and for sales forces in situations where distances preclude social interaction among sales reps. A well-produced, glossy monthly newsletter, especially designed for the sales force, containing business-unit news, promotions, marriages, births, and outstanding sales accomplishments can foster feelings of belonging, recognition, and pride. Following are several guidelines for successful sales newsletters:

☐ Keep the technical and product content to a minimum and the social and personal-recognition content to a maximum.

☐ Mail the newsletter to the sales rep's home, and make sure it's full of names and faces.

☐ If the success of your sales force depends heavily on liaison with service, distribution, and other internal personnel, include them in the newsletter, too.

If it's fun to read and up-to-date, a sales-force newsletter can give you a lot of bang for your motivational buck.

SALES CONTESTS

Caution: This section is not applicable if competition among your sales reps or your sales districts is not desirable. Sales contests can provide—under the proper circumstances—great short- and long-term incentives to perform and opportunities for recognition. They can backfire, however, if they are used under conditions where cooperation among sales reps and sales districts or liaison among several business-unit functions are key to the success of your sales operation.

Sales contests usually take two forms: (1) contests used to help achieve short-term results, solve specific problems, or drum up interest and enthusiasm in normally slow periods and (2) contests used to establish incentives and recognition over longer time periods. These latter (usually annual) sales contests are discussed more fully later, under Sales Standings.

Some of the following circumstances prevent short-term sales contests from being effective:

☐ They are held too frequently. Thus, your sales reps come to expect them on a regular basis, and the excitement quickly wears off.

☐ They are held too regularly. This condition can lead to "bagging," saving orders and turning them in when the next (and predictable) contest period starts.

☐ The prizes are too trivial or too costly. The latter condition happens more frequently than you might think. I recall one instance when a sales rep won an all-expense-paid week with her spouse in Hawaii. The cost of the prize was greater than the gross-margin contribution from all the goods sold during the contest period. "Ouch!" said the controller.

☐ The same people tend to win all the contests, a condition that suggests favoritism toward the few and leads to lethargy among the many.

Some of the ways these problems can be avoided are illustrated by the following example.

THE POKER CONTEST

A district manager has six sales reps. A contest is established to sell more service contracts (the business unit's short-term problem at the moment). The dollar value of a service contract is calculated. Each member of the sales district is dealt a hole card face down that is pasted next to his or her name on a poster in the district office. The sales rep does not know what card he or she holds. For each service contract sold, the sales rep receives a card that is pasted face up on the poster board. The contest is over when the last card has been dealt out.

When 46 service contracts have been sold, the prize is awarded, not necessarily to the sales rep who sold the most service contracts, but to the one with the best poker hand once the hole cards have been turned up. The contest is "over when it's over." Although one's chances improve with each card earned, four queens beats a five-card straight. And no one knows who is going to win until the hole cards are exposed. Thus, interest is sustained throughout the period.

The cost of the prize is less than the dollar contribution from 46 incremental service contracts.

SALES STANDINGS

Sales standings have some of the same drawbacks as sales contests: The same people outdistance the pack and earn all the rewards. The same caution also applies to sales standings as applies to sales contests: Use a public list only when you desire to foster competition. Sales standings, particularly when published in your newsletter, are a powerful form of recognition and a useful tool to promote voluntary resignations on the part of your marginal performers.

The keys to effective use of sales standings are the use of multiple criteria and substantial reward and recognition. The use of multiple criteria to establish sales standings is illustrated in the following example.

SALES STANDINGS BASED ON MULTIPLE CRITERIA

The sales force used in this illustration comprises about 150 sales reps who are assigned to one of six or seven districts in each of four regions.

Each month, every sales rep is ranked in four categories: (1) cumulative year-to-date sales (which rewards the top performers); (2) percentage gain over same month last year (which rewards the emerging top performers); (3) percentage cumulative gain against a territory buying-power index as measured by an outside source (which rewards late bloomers and those weaker sales reps who are trying hard, but makes it harder for top performers to score well here because they have already squeezed their turnip hard); and (4) a special category chosen monthly—such as sale of service contracts or accessories—which rewards anybody who cooperates in these special situations.

The sales reps are ranked from top to bottom based on the fewest points (as in golf) to accommodate changes in the size of the sales force. As the fiscal year goes on, the monthly standings are averaged to develop an average cumulative monthly standing (ACM)—a tactic that encourages consistency of effort and acts as a buffer against windfalls and catastrophes.

Sales reps with fewer than 12 months' service ("rookies") are rated on separate scales.

The ACM standings are published in a monthly newsletter, which provides recognition for the Eagles and others showing improvement and a motive for the weak performers to seek employment elsewhere.

At the end of the fiscal year, based on the final ACM standings, the top 10 sales reps, the top rookie, and their respective district managers (the managers' reward for developing sales results) win an all-expense-paid trip to the Super Bowl. The top sales rep and top district manager in each region (their reward for sales results) win a two-week trip with spouses or "significant others" to some glamorous vacation spot, usually overseas.

Despite the multiple criteria, which tend to compress the point spread and therefore keep more sales reps striving for the substantial rewards and recognition involved, the Eagles tend to be the winners by year-end because of their consistency in cumulative sales, percentage gain over last year (although a tough challenge), and performance in the monthly special categories.

SALES CONVENTIONS

Marvelous if you can afford them, the costs of sales conventions aren't usually hard to justify if you run them well. If you have a first-class product line, a first-class management team, and a first-class sales force, you can probably afford a first-class sales convention.

Where should you hold the convention? In a first-class resort setting.

When should you go? Annually. But remember, sales conventions become a fixed cost. After a good year and a sales convention in Bermuda, it is disastrous to announce in a slow year that we're going to whoop it up in Acne, USA.

How long should it last? Give everyone Friday to travel there. Have fun on Saturday, Sunday, Monday, and Tuesday. Give everyone Wednesday to travel back.

What should you do? The Internal Revenue Service wants its pound of flesh, so take Monday and Tuesday mornings for "business meetings." Use the rest of the time for recreation.

What should you not do? Avoid training sessions, an activity best done at other times and places. Avoid evening speeches, especially those containing exhortations to "work harder." Use the evenings for entertainment and for recognizing individual and team performances.

Who should get to go? Sales conventions provide great opportunities for communication, morale boosting, and team building. Invite all sales reps, sales managers, and marketing managers. If your sales reps are in frequent telephone or personal contact with service and distribution people, invite them too: A sales rep who calls in with a service problem will get a better reception on the other end of the line if the service person is someone with whom he or she has played golf. Don't forget spouses or significant others. Don't invite customers. They tend to get in the way of everyone relaxing and having fun.

Many executives are hesitant to bestow special incentives on one part of the organization and exclude others. (The plant people don't attend lavish conventions; why should the sales reps?) Sales reps do not typically enjoy a built-in social system, however, as office workers and plant personnel do. The sales rep's job can be lonely and at times the work environment can be hostile (such as dealing with irate customers). The sales rep is the company to the many people who deal with the company as customers. The sales rep is the one employee charged with the responsibility of implementing business strategy under conditions of extreme reality: face-to-face on the customer's home turf. Don't sales reps deserve special attention?

SALES MEETINGS

If you want a quick sales meeting, remove all the chairs. If you want a good one, publish the agenda beforehand and stick to it.

Some bad reasons for holding sales meetings are (1) to criticize group and/or individual accomplishment and (2) to "get together" on a regular basis.

Some good reasons for holding sales meetings are (1) to praise group and/or individual accomplishments, (2) to disseminate ideas and information, and (3) to collect ideas and information.

Your managers should have a good reason for pulling your sales reps in from the field. Every minute they're not selling is costing you money. The bad reasons suggest regular meetings held every 100 years. The good reasons suggest irregular meetings held as frequently as necessary.

NEWTON'S LAWS

XI. Only the lead dog gets a change of scenery.

Chapter 14

Performance Appraisal

My suspicion is that the vast majority of sales organizations that use formal annual performance appraisals use them to justify (legally and otherwise) terminating people. It seems to me that good field management—frequent on-the-job training visits and candid and informal evaluation of the sales rep's performance on the spot—provides the best opportunity to praise and encourage high performance, and correct bad habits before they become ingrained. Sales reps need and want frequent opportunities to discuss their performance. Communicating performance against expectations and planning for improvement are too important to be left to periodic (and often traumatic) rituals. For many managers, conducting an annual performance appraisal with subordinates is the single most unpleasant, difficult, and generally unproductive task among their many job responsibilities.

Nevertheless, formal performance-appraisal systems do exist, and many sales executives claim that a good performance appraisal system can be the single most important tool in improving sales-force performance. Thus, sales executives need to be concerned about, and need to have their own system for, evaluating the performance of the individuals reporting to them—and their own performance. Evaluation criteria can range from pure sales-volume gains to return-on-investment calculations. Evaluation criteria can range from the highly subjective to the totally quantitative. Judgments must be carefully made in full awareness that your decisions about how people are evaluated have enormous impact on how they behave.

Many sales executives have come to recognize that the performance-appraisal system itself can create major problems for the average field sales manager. For instance, consider these typical burdens placed on the appraiser by some performance-appraisal systems:

☐ The need to appraise performance along dimensions that are irrelevant to the actual requirements of the job. ("Who cares if he uses crude language occasionally? He's the best salesman I've got.")

☐ The need to appraise personal attributes, an activity that trained psychologists have difficulty doing well. ("How do I know how 'loyal' she is to the company?")

☐ The need to communicate these appraisals of personal traits to a potentially hostile listener. ("How do I explain my reasons for giving him a 'seven' on 'Exercises Good Judgment'?")

☐ The need to conduct and communicate a comprehensive recounting of the subordinates' accomplishments in the past year and—euphemistically—their "areas for improvement." ("Do I really need to remind her how upset I was last August when she failed to get that report in on time?")

Not only have these traditional appraisal systems complicated the appraisal task for the individual manager, but such formal systems increasingly also fail to meet EEOC and other fair-employment guidelines that require the use of objective performance criteria in decisions affecting promotion, transfer, training, or retention. Thus, many high-performance sales organizations have shifted their performance-appraisal systems and philosophies in the following directions:

☐ From a focus on personality traits to a focus on job-related behavior and results.

☐ From an emphasis on recounting past peccadilloes to an emphasis on developing future action plans.

☐ From viewing performance appraisal as an annual ritual to viewing appraisal as an ongoing process.

☐ From a focus on static job descriptions to a focus on specific task requirements identified by systematic job analysis.

☐ From a focus on evaluation to a focus on development.

☐ From unilateral appraisals to bilateral discussions.

PROBATION

Related to performance appraisal, and sometimes its consequence, is the practice of putting someone on "probation." This situation occurs in some sales organizations when the individual has covertly given up (probably long ago) and the sales manager (acting for the organization) overtly gives up. For example:

> "Mary's a good gal but she just can't hack it. I guess we better put her on 90-day probation before we let her go."

Why can't Mary "hack it," and why had we "better put her on 90-day probation"? Maybe Mary can't hack it because she's learned how to be helpless. Maybe she's overqualified (and bored) or underqualified (and frustrated). Anyway, her lethargy has reached the point where a manager's lethargy has become unbearable, so the organization agrees to "put her on probation." If the manager is "playing fair," he or she sets some "objective" standards for Mary to meet and informs her that she will be "[ex]terminated" if these standards are not met within 90 days. What does that sentence mean?

To Mary, it can mean: (1) a big sticky, gooey, smelly, foul brown chip; (2) her desire for recognition has finally been satisfied (although not too pleasantly)—she is now "somebody," (although just barely); (3) a 90-day paid vacation with lots of opportunities to retaliate with a few brown chips of her own; (4) a 90-day paid vacation with lots of opportunities to look for another job; (5) a 90-day paid vacation with lots of opportunities to talk to her lawyer; or (6) all of 1 through 5.

The possibility that Mary will "come off" probation is remote, particularly if the probationary standards have been "properly" set (that is, not even Wonder Woman could meet them). Even if she does survive this probationary period, the possibility that Mary will become a productive and committed employee in the future is even more remote. Chances are that Mary will either quit (with a bad taste in her mouth) or get fired (with all the attendant possibilities of legal action), and 90 days of her life will have been wasted. As with learned helplessness (discussed in Part IV), probation rarely leads to anything but an "everybody loses" outcome. Counseling out (discussed in Part III) is a much better technique for low performers.

TERMINATION

Related to probation, and often its consequence, is the practice of termination. Unless your managers really enjoy being a witness or a defendant in a court trial, they should be aware of the legal aspects of employee termination. The laws change constantly, but they increasingly become more situational in application and make justifying the termination of an employee more difficult. State labor laws differ from one state to another, tend to be stricter than federal labor laws, and cover enterprises with fewer than the 15-employee federal limit. As a consequence, your managers should never presume to know the law but should know when to seek legal advice.

In general, however, you may not terminate an employee for reasons of expediency. These reasons include (but are not restricted to) discrimination (racial, sexual, and so on), retaliation (for example, against "whistle blowers"), and violation of public policy (such as attempts to force an employee to disregard rules regarding public safety).

Further, in general you may not terminate an employee if the *motive* for termination fails to exhibit good faith and fair dealing. For example, the laws side against you if the criteria for termination are not widely and plainly communicated, the criteria are selectively enforced, the criteria are difficult to quantify, or the criteria are not applied fairly to the specifics of the termination decision. One extreme example of the latter situation is the so-called "constructive discharge," which forces an employee to resign by structuring intolerable working conditions (such as an unacceptable transfer or a desk in the boiler room).

In general, you may terminate an employee if the *motive* can be shown to be economic. Employees who are hired for an indefinite period without a formal employment contract or collective bargaining agreement can be terminated for the following (not inclusive) reasons: inadequate job performance, failure to adhere to company policies or work rules, unsatisfactory behavior having no implications beyond the work place, and business necessity (such as "down-sizing"). Obviously, these reasons must be carefully documented.

The process for terminating an employee should include the following procedures:

Continuing Appraisal

Sales reps, particularly new ones, need feedback on a frequent and continuing basis on how they are doing compared with the criteria on which they are judged.

Early Warning

Sales reps are entitled to an early oral warning that their performance is unsatisfactory and are entitled to counseling in ways to improve that performance.

Written Warning

If the unsatisfactory performance is not showing sufficient improvement, additional counseling and a written warning should be provided within some reasonable period after the oral warning—say, two weeks, if that is a practical span for collecting the necessary data. The written warning should include a description of the unsatisfactory behavior; notification of the consequences to the sales rep and to the business unit if this behavior is not improved; a set of desired actions to be taken on the part of the sales rep to correct and improve that behavior; (ideally) a set of actions to be taken on the part of the field manager to help correct and improve that behavior; (ideally) quantifiable goals to be met reflecting satisfactory performance; and a specific target date to accomplish those goals.

Final Warning

If the written goals are not met, a final written warning should be given to the sales rep informing him or her that a probationary period is in effect. The notification should contain a deadline for meeting specific performance goals, details of the areas for improvement, and relevant measurement criteria. The warning should state that failure to achieve the performance goals by the end of the probationary period will result in termination.

Dismissal

After concurrence from you, your manager should inform the sales rep in private and with as much tact and compassion as possible—that he or she has failed to meet the conditions of his or her probation and is therefore terminated. Ideally, the termination procedures and techniques should be perceived as being fair, even-handed, and dignified. And even more ideally, the sales rep will concur with the decision.

Except in rare incidents, the necessity to terminate an employee is a sign of management failure. Either the employee has been poorly recruited, selected, trained, or motivated or the management personnel are deficient in interpersonal or policy-making skills. In high-performance sales organizations, incompetent people receive insufficient reward for staying on the job, but are treated with dignity and respect and counseled out with the view that their latent competence will enable them to grow and develop in another work situation. In high-performance sales organizations competent people are provided with an opportunity to grow, develop, and flourish.

TURNOVER

Resignations and terminations produce employee turnover. For executives in low-performance sales organizations, turnover can cause panic. For executives in high-performance sales organizations, turnover can provide opportunities for even higher performance.

The Bureau of Labor Statistics (BLS) formula for calculating employee turnover is:

$$\frac{\text{Quits and Discharges}}{(\text{Total workers on January 1} + \text{Total workers on Dec. 31})/2}$$

When this figure, applied to your sales force, exceeds 10 percent, you are probably running a costly sales force. Your recruiting, training, and empty-territory (opportunity-loss) costs are high. It obviously pays to hire Eagles and feed them well. High sales-force turnover (for most industries defined as exceeding 10 percent) does not necessarily equate to low levels of performance, however. It depends on *where* the turnover is coming from. The ideal situation manifested in many high-performance sales forces is this pattern:

☐ Top third of sales force: no quits; some promotions.

☐ Middle third of sales force: some quits.

☐ Bottom third of sales force: lots of quits.

☐ No discharges—marginal producers are counseled out.

If your managers are losing their top people and holding onto their marginal ones, something is awry. Usually this situation is caused by misallocation or insufficiency of your field sales managers' time. To have your managers spend a great deal of time working in the field with their best sales reps tends to reduce turnover among your Eagles by providing them with the evidence that they are valued (they need tender, loving care as much as other birds). Because most of your results come from your Eagles, and your Eagles are characteristically interested in becoming even better, encouraging your field sales managers to work more with their Eagles usually results in a better return on their managerial investment than trying to rescue their marginal performers. Feeding your Eagles lowers turnover where you want low turnover, raises turnover where you want high turnover (the turkeys are starved out), and raises the overall performance of the business unit.

If you substitute "transfers and promotions" for "quits and discharges" in the BLS formula, you get what I call your "opportunity rate." It tends to correlate *positively* with your turnover rate and is considered high when it exceeds 5 percent. This research-verified phenomenon may be counterintuitive to managers who believe that high opportunity means low turnover and high performance. Nevertheless, particularly in larger sales forces (with more than 250 people), performance of the sales task may be perceived as the pathway to promotion. When a sales rep fails to receive one, he or she quits in favor of another opportunity elsewhere. Low opportunity rates are usually characteristic of a stable, "professional" sales force whose personnel are dedicated to performing the sales task well and perceive a possible promotion to be the reward for their performance (as opposed to a stimulus for them to perform well). But your opportunity rate is not to be taken as a value judgment: a high opportunity rate may be a function of your business unit's strategy (particularly in high-growth situations); a low opportunity rate may be a sign of stagnation.

NEWTON'S LAWS

XII. You don't get paid for effort.
You get paid for results.

Chapter 15

The Invisible Supervisor

Leadership, the management of motivation, includes the determination of policies and procedures to gain spontaneous and reasoned support for your business unit's mission and to facilitate the implementation of your business-unit and sales-force strategy. Furthermore, the management system—this collection of policies and procedures—must satisfy at least four criteria.

First, your management system must provide a working climate conducive to the accomplishment of your business unit's objectives. For most high-performance sales forces, this criterion means providing your Eagles with the opportunity to excel: not bogging them down with useless activities, such as writing reports; not clipping their wings by setting boundaries or ceilings on their selling activities, such as arbitrary quotas or anachronistic performance standards; and not taking them for granted by ignoring their requirements for top-flight training and supervision.

Second, your management system must provide "understood meanings," which ensure that both the letter and the spirit of your policies and procedures are observed as your marketing and selling tasks are performed. When your sales reps feel well and fairly treated—for example, when sales reps see that compensation plans and appraisal systems do indeed reward the Eagles and discourage the turkeys—they will tend to pay more attention to the "invisible supervisor," the values that influence the quality and quantity of the work your sales organization performs.

Third, your management system must encourage the personal growth and development of your sales reps. When your Eagles see that their activities and efforts are recognized and rewarded (and therefore have value to them) and that their activities and efforts make a contribution to the business unit (and therefore have value to you), your management system will have achieved goal congruence, a vital objective in managing motivation.

Fourth, your management system should encourage feelings of cooperation and team spirit among your sales reps and between them and other members of your business unit. For many high-performance sales forces, the nature of the sales task and the natural consequence of multiple interactions among sales reps, service personnel, and other business-unit personnel foster cooperation and team spirit. For other high-performance sales forces, however, the sales reps' personal-growth and development opportunities may conflict with the business unit's requirements for cooperation and team spirit. This aspect of managing motivation requires continuous monitoring to protect the business unit from falling prey to the competing interests of individual and group achievement. On the one hand, your Eagles need wide latitude to achieve high altitude. On the other hand, your management system must ensure that your business unit fulfills its key commitments.

Leadership involves the definition of desired behavior and the design of a management system that *encourages* sales reps to conform to that behavior. No management system, however, can guarantee conformity. Part III of this book discusses the role of field sales managers as they work to *ensure* that behavior.

PART III

THE MANAGERS:
CLIMATE AND STYLE

Chapter 16

Field Supervision

In high-performance sales organizations field sales managers develop in their people a sense of shared purpose and genuine commitment to fulfilling the mission of the business unit. These managers recognize that high levels of shared purpose and commitment are achieved when people view their own activities within the organization as satisfying their own needs to grow and develop. Whereas well-conceived organizational policies can encourage desired behavior, executives in high-performance sales forces look to their field sales managers to ensure that behavior. In that sense, field sales managers are teachers, people who attempt to close the gap between actual behavior (what people do) and desired behavior (what the business unit is striving to have them do). Teaching is a vital ingredient in managing motivation.

THE ROLE OF THE FIELD SALES MANAGER

A clear mission, a soundly conceived yet responsive strategy, and a management system that encourages behavior consistent with the execution of that strategy help produce a working climate that attracts competent people and stimulates and rewards them to perform their sales tasks well. The role of the field sales manager in this process can be diagramed as shown in Figure 4.

Environmental forces create organizational opportunities (and threats). The strategic process determines the organizational responses to these forces. The management system supports and implements the decisions that flow from the strategic process. The values of key executives (the strategy makers) determine which strategic options are chosen—distinguishing the desirable from the merely doable—and influence the design of the various elements of the management system so as to encourage the appropriate behavior on the part of the organization's members. The workplace climate is created in part by the management system and in part by the managers' styles as they administer policies and influence the behavior of their people. Competent people are attracted to this workplace climate because they perceive that the combination of organizational mission, strategy, management system, and personal style of the managers is conducive to helping them satisfy their own workplace and personal needs. High task performance is the consequence of these carefully thought-out relationships. The area within the dotted line represents this style-climate-people-task relationship. Your field sales managers' responsibility is to make this relationship work. It's their role in managing motivation.

In low-performance organizations, environmental forces are ignored or misread. The strategic process produces decisions that lead to aimless drift or short-run opportunism. The management system is

FIGURE 4

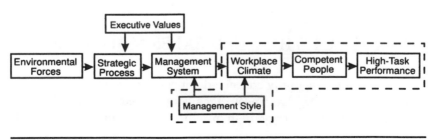

characterized by the search for Magic Bananas or secured rigidly in place by attitudes such as "This is the way we've always done it." Executive values contribute little of worth to the organization's sense of direction or purpose. The workplace climate fosters trips to lethargy. Managerial behavior provokes "Nobody cares about me or the work I do" feelings. Incompetents get rewarded, and tasks are performed at minimally acceptable standards (to both boss and subordinate).

In high-performance organizations, environmental forces are monitored and analyzed. The strategic process produces decisions that further enhance the business unit's competitive position and viability. The management system encourages innovation and sensible risk-taking. Executive values have economic utility to the business unit and personal utility to its members. The workplace climate fosters a commitment to high performance. Managerial behavior stimulates cooperation, communication, and personal growth and development. Competent people receive the rewards and work gets performed willingly, cheerfully, and at levels that surprise and delight boss and subordinate alike.

BARRIERS TO EFFECTIVE FIELD SUPERVISION

Your field sales managers should be led to recognize that their primary responsibility is to encourage conformity between actual behavior (what sales reps do) and desired behavior (what you want them to do). This important position is often the Achilles heel of the sales force. It is critical in managing motivation. Good field sales management requires (1) a properly defined job that permits the manager to spend enough time performing appropriate field training and supervisory activities to get results and (2) personal behavior that meets the coaching and counseling needs of subordinates and encourages them to high performance.

The lack of adequate field supervision is a common complaint among sales reps, their customers, and even senior managers. One reason for this lack is the widely held belief that experienced sales reps—and Eagles in particular—do not need supervision or will not stand for it. "Sales reps should be treated as if they were in business for themselves," many managers assume. According to this view, mature sales reps—particularly those paid on straight commission—when left alone, will act in their own self-interest and maximize their own and the business unit's sales volume.

Marketing strategies nowadays, however, are too dynamic and complex to permit sales reps to act merely in their own self-interest. Most sales organizations require sales reps to perform many activities that fall outside a definition of self-interest. Your managers should recognize that sales reps are seldom in business for themselves; they are hired to implement your marketing strategy. Furthermore, lack of supervision is particularly damaging to your Eagles, who want to do even better, and whose efforts are all too often taken for granted.

A second reason for inadequate field supervision is that sales executives often fail to define the field sales manager's job properly. Field sales managers and executives alike often do not recognize that the field sales manager's key tasks involve observing actual sales-force behavior and working to improve it in the field.

Instead of giving highest priority to supervisory tasks, some business units assign field sales managers their own customers to handle—either because "it's good for them to keep their hands in" or because the size or importance of the accounts seems to warrant their receiving a manager's attention. This practice can cause field sales managers to overemphasize their own selling activities at the expense of developing the skills of their sales reps—particularly if the managers' incomes and performance appraisals depend on their success with their own accounts.

Other sales organizations, rather than seeing their managers as primarily sales reps, see them as primarily administrators. This attitude causes field sales managers to become bogged down with paperwork, report writing, and other duties better left to specialists—activities such as reconciling expense accounts or conducting customer surveys. Assigning any administrative task to your field sales managers should always be considered a tradeoff: Is this administrative task worth depriving your managers of time in the field to work with their sales reps?

Often, newly promoted field sales managers are well aware that field supervision should be their first priority, but they may be uncertain how to supervise. One reason for such uncertainty is their own lack of training. Many sales organizations routinely promote their best sales reps to management without adequately preparing them for their new responsibilities. Success as a sales rep does not guarantee success as a manager. Unless the selling job had a great deal of managerial content—such as a job in which planning, coordinating, and integrating the tasks of many people are critical to consummating the sale—most sales reps find that managing other people's activities requires different skills from asking a customer for an order. Indeed, in many sales organizations, the super sales rep is often the least likely to be a good planner, a good organizer, or a good delegator. Furthermore, the super sales rep is often unaware of the reasons for his or her success and, thus, is unable to coach and direct the behavior of others.

A second reason for new managers' uncertainty is that many sales executives fail to communicate their objectives (desired behavior) for the sales force. Not only must you define for your field sales managers the precise role sales reps are to play in your business unit's marketing strategy, you must also update that definition every time changes in the competitive environment force changes in your marketing strategy. If current desired behavior is not understood, field sales managers will direct their sales reps to perform as they always have or, even worse, to perform as they performed when they were sales reps. Unless the activities of the sales force conform to the desired behavior, your sales force will be doing one thing while you are expecting another. On the other hand, once your field sales managers understand the sales force's role in the business unit's marketing strategy, they can provide the kind of supervision appropriate to this role and to the needs of their individual sales reps. The caliber of field supervision is an integral component in managing motivation, because the behavior of your field sales managers has an important bearing on how your sales reps feel about the work they do.

FIXIT MANAGEMENT

Jagdish Teja, a friend of mine and a practicing psychiatrist, claims that American managers suffer from the "handyman syndrome." I call it "fixit management." It's a disorder endemic in business organizations, because managers are paid to fix stuff. They are evaluated on their ability to fix stuff. They go to work in the morning looking for opportunities to fix stuff. If they don't find an opportunity to fix stuff, they come home at night feeling guilty ("I got paid for doing nothing"), anxious ("Maybe I missed something"), and fearful ("What if I missed something and someone finds out?"). If two or three days go by without an opportunity to fix stuff (to demonstrate to others their managerial talent), real terror sets in:

"They don't need me."

"I'm losing my touch."

"I'll get passed over."

"They'll transfer me."

"Maybe they'll even fire me."

Fixit management is so entrenched in the organizational way of life that no one can escape its effects. All entry-level jobs involve fixing stuff (from sweeping floors to handling customer problems, from mailing out bills to oiling machinery). And people are told that to get ahead they must show initiative (find more stuff to fix), demonstrate responsibility (fix stuff right), creativity (fix stuff better), and dependability (fix the stuff you're told to fix). When people get promoted, they are often sent to "management development" seminars where they are taught analytical skills (how to recognize what stuff needs fixing), technical skills (the mechanics of fixing stuff), and "human" skills (how to get other people to fix stuff).

In order to make fixit management work, it's necessary to find something going wrong; otherwise, there's nothing to fix. That part is easy; the manager has been trained, remember? Generally, when something is going wrong, at least one other person is involved—usually someone who is "responsible" for it (but an innocent by-stander will do). The first move, of course, is for the manager to point out to the people involved that "something" is wrong and it's their "fault." In Armed Services jargon, this maneuver is called "Kicking Ass and Taking Names" (KATN). Despite the manager's technical competence ("Here's what's wrong") and human relations skills ("Let me show you how to fix it"), the damage has been done: An attempt has been made to make someone feel crummy. If your managers can keep this activity up all day long, your sales reps will be miserable, and the quantity and quality of work produced will be marginal at best. The only reward for fixit management is that, if your managers do find enough stuff to fix, they can go home at five o'clock secure in the belief that they have put in a day's work.

Fixit management is a consequence of ignorance (the manager doesn't know any better), expedience (the manager doesn't have the time to do it any better), or pressure (the manager can't afford to make mistakes). Fixit management is also the course of least resis-tance. Finding stuff that needs fixing is a lot easier than looking for stuff that's going right—an activity for which few managers are trained and none is paid.

Only for satisfying the most basic needs do guilt, anxiety, and fear serve as motivators, and not too effective ones at that. Fixit man-agement tends to discourage authentic behavior, derail productiv-ity, and stop the process of personal growth and development dead in its tracks.

Your managers should spend their time looking for stuff that's going right, and they should spend time recognizing and compli-menting those responsible. Managers who improve the workplace climate for their sales reps also improve the quantity and quality of the sales activities performed. Help your managers avoid becoming fixit managers. Encourage them to look for things going right and get them to recognize and reward high performance when they see it. Managing motivation properly demands these kinds of management behaviors.

NEWTON'S LAWS

XIII. Take care of your people and the numbers will
take care of themselves.

Rader

Chapter 17

Climate

The workplace is a subset of the culture of your organization. Corporate culture does not refer to the sculptures and paintings displayed in the lobby of your company's headquarters nor the quality of the music in your elevator. It is a powerful, yet unseen and tacit, force that influences your behavior and the behavior of the people who report to you. It includes all the understood meanings, interpersonal protocols, and institutional mores that define the attitudes and activities of the people who get ahead in your organization as opposed to those who don't.

When people talk about corporate culture, they make comments such as:

"Every man here wears a coat and tie to work. Even the women wear suits."

"We're on a first-name basis around here except for Mr. Bedlam. He's the president."

"One of the things you just don't do around here is get to a meeting late."

"Of course I work overtime. It's expected."

"We don't have contracts with our suppliers. Everything is done by handshake."

"Women get treated pretty good around here. Why, we've even got a few on the sales force."

In many organizations, to violate these cultural dictates is to doom one's career. Cultures that encourage growth, creativity, and excellence can produce extraordinary levels of performance, job satisfaction, and loyalty. Cultures that reward the status quo, ritualistic behavior, and mediocrity get what they deserve. If your culture is a positive force, teach those meanings, protocols, and mores to the people who report to you. If it isn't, do what you can to change the culture or get out.

Culture is a powerful force in influencing performance levels because it influences the behavior of the social units that people tend to form within the organization. These social units have objectives, strategies, rules, standards, leaders, and hierarchical relationships that may differ from those of the organizations within which they work. Managing motivation effectively, therefore, requires that your managers understand the relationships between and among people in order to channel the energies created by these "informal" organizations into complementing the activities of the "formal" organization. These group dynamics contribute to the climate of people's workplaces, which, in turn, influence their performance and job satisfaction.

Simply stated, climate refers to people's perceptions of what their workplace "feels" like, how they describe those feelings, and how those feelings influence their desire to perform well. To describe the climate of their workplace, people make such comments as:

"There's a lot of red tape here."

"If you don't perform, you're out."

"People here feel good about one another."

"They really encourage you here to do it your own way."

"The only way to get recognized around here is to screw up."

"We all pull together here; it makes everyone work hard."

"The harder you work here, the more dough you can make."

"I do my best work when I'm left alone. Nobody bugs me here."

Some of these comments suggest that the climate can be a negative influence on performance. Others suggest that the climate can be a positive influence. Still others suggest that the climate can cause some people to be turned off and others to be turned on.

Much of the variability in these responses can be accounted for by the variability in people's relative needs. One person's "red tape" is another person's "security." One person's "pressure" is another person's "challenge." Thus, it's hard to describe a climate as "good" or "bad."

CLIMATE VARIABLES

Nevertheless, to bring out the best in their people, your field sales managers need to attempt to match people's needs with climates that encourage them to perform well. A number of researchers have studied the characteristics of people who tend to perform well in particular work climates. The ideas that emerge from these studies generally suggest (but with no consensus) the following matchings.

Structure: the degree to which people feel guided or directed by specific policies and procedures. Some people, particularly those with high needs for affiliation, feel uncomfortable in highly structured situations, because they object to things being "run by the book." Other people, particularly those with high needs for achievement, will tolerate some structure in their job if they perceive that those rules and regulations support their activities and that the absence of structure would lead to chaos and disorganization. People with high needs for power usually welcome high structure, because it can provide opportunities to advance in a formal hierarchy, thus satisfying their need to gain status and control over others.

Responsibility: the degree to which people perceive delegation. Some people, particularly those with high needs for achievement, welcome situations that give them the feeling that they can run their own show. They chafe in situations that produce feelings that no one can do anything without someone else's approval. Other people, including many with high needs for affiliation, neither seek responsibility nor want it, preferring to go along with the crowd. People with high needs for power tend to seek responsibility because it represents status and a means for becoming more visible within the organization.

Risk: the degree to which people feel encouraged to take chances and enjoy the rewards and suffer the consequences of doing things their way. People with high needs for achievement enjoy taking calculated risks. People with high needs for affiliation and power generally don't; it is more important for them to avoid mistakes than to do things on their own.

Standards: the degree to which people feel pressure to perform well. Some people, particularly those with high needs for achievement, welcome situations that demand reasonably high standards of performance, because these situations provide challenge and competition. Other people, particularly those with high needs for affiliation, prefer standards that foster low levels of individual competitiveness and high levels of group interaction. People with high needs for power are often indifferent to standards, preferring to challenge others rather than be challenged themselves.

Rewards: the degree to which people feel their performance is recognized. People with high needs for achievement tend to seek recognition for achieving their goals; people with high needs for affiliation tend to seek the approval of other people; people with high needs for power tend to seek status, position, and other tangible evidence of accomplishment, such as stripes, medals, and prominent spaces in the parking lot.

Support: the degree to which people feel other people help and encourage them to perform well. People with high needs for achievement and affiliation generally welcome support in the workplace. In the former instance, support helps the achievers gain their objectives; in the latter, it makes the affiliators feel like part of a team. People with high needs for power may be indifferent to support because it goes against their "be strong" values.

Conflict: the degree to which people feel that differences of opinion are encouraged and constructively resolved. People with high needs for achievement tend to welcome dealing with and resolving issues of consequence to them. People with high needs for affiliation tend to prefer to leave argument and confrontation to other people. People with high needs for power tend to enjoy argument and confrontation, particularly when they "win."

Warmth: the degree to which people feel friendliness and closeness toward the people around them. People with high needs for achievement generally welcome a warm work atmosphere, because it represents a hassle-free environment within which they can do their thing. It's an even more important factor, however, for those with high needs for affiliation, because friendliness and closeness are their primary needs. For people with high needs for power, personal warmth in the workplace may make them uncomfortable: today's buddy may become tomorrow's boss.

Group Identity: the degree to which people perceive that the workplace exudes team spirit. People with high needs for achievement usually welcome identification with a winning team so long as they don't feel swallowed up by the achievements of their group. People with high needs for affiliation enjoy being a part of the team. People with high needs for power tend to take pride in the groups with which they identify, because belonging to the right groups is an important source of their status.

These dimensions have been grouped and regrouped by researchers seeking to match climates in a neat and precise way with people's needs for achievement, affiliation, and power. It's hard to do. Furthermore, to describe, for example, a person as having a high need for achievement, one must remember that need is relative, both to that person's needs for affiliation and power and to other people's needs for achievement.

Nevertheless, most studies suggest that people with high needs for achievement will tend to perform better within a climate of high responsibility, risk, and standards. People with high needs for affiliation will tend to perform better within a climate of warmth, support, and group identity. And people with high needs for power will tend to perform better within a climate of structure, responsibility, and conflict (resolution). Surface generalities aren't enough, however. Superficial analyses of people's needs and task requirements can be misleading. Although to conclude that all good sales reps have high needs for achievement is easy, many sales reps (for example, those selling highly technical products to small groups of sophisticated customers) have higher needs for affiliation than for achievement. At the other extreme, many sales reps (for example, those selling encyclopedias door-to-door) often have high needs for power (control over others) and high needs for achievement, but very low needs for affiliation.

Seldom does a sales force comprise people with similar relative needs for achievement, affiliation, and power. Knowledge of the specifics of the tasks required of your particular sales force and understanding the relationship between your sales reps' needs and their perceptions of climate can help you and your managers get beyond surface generalities. Your field sales managers' behavior can have a substantial impact on how their sales reps feel about their workplace climate and how those feelings influence their performance. The next chapter discusses the relationship between your field sales managers' behavior and the workplace climate variables.

NEWTON'S LAWS

XIV. You'll never get ahead until your people get behind you.

Chapter 18

Style

A person's style is a collection of other peoples' descriptions of that person's behavior. When your managers say and do things, they define for other people who they are and what they are like. These definitions are a function of other people's reality. Thus, your managers' styles—how their behavior is perceived and described by others—is beyond their total control. You can only hope that their efforts to treat their sales reps with consideration, understanding, and fairness will produce an accurate concensual reputation.

To the degree that people can control how other people perceive them, your field sales managers' behavior can have a significant influence on how their sales reps perceive the workplace climate. Because people have a great deal of freedom in choosing how they respond to various situations, in their role as managers people can exercise similar degrees of freedom. Here are some examples of the dimensions of managerial behavior that can have an impact on how sales reps perceive the workplace climate.

Coaching

How much time and effort do your managers spend teaching people? What do they teach them: Technical aspects of their job? Interpersonal aspects? or "The Big Picture"? For what part of their sales reps' personal growth and development are your managers taking responsibility?

Standards

How important is it for your managers to set and communicate standards of performance? How high should they be set? How should they be measured and monitored? What feedback mechanisms are desirable? How frequently should your managers provide feedback, both formally and informally? What happens if the standards aren't met?

Delegation

How much responsibility do your managers give their sales reps for performing their tasks as they see fit? What are the purposes of delegation: to foster initiative, creativity, or a sense of ownership? When should conditions of urgency, risk, or uniformity cause your managers to overrule normal conditions of delegation?

Freedom

How much risk should your managers encourage their sales reps to take? What are the penalties for failure? The rewards for success? What support systems are in place to ensure that one sales rep's failure doesn't generate risk aversion among the others?

Decision Making

What is the desired process for making decisions? Is it unilateral and directive or mutual and participative? Should your managers encourage or suppress differences of opinion? Should they try to resolve differences of opinion quickly, or should these conflicts be allowed to dissolve over time?

Praise and Criticism

How do your managers handle praise and criticism with their sales reps? What conditions merit praise? What conditions merit criticism?

Flexibility

How well do your managers adapt their behavior to circumstances and to individual differences among their people? What is the tradeoff between consistency in behavior and flexibility? Between "fairness" and flexibility? Between predictability and flexibility?

Personal Distance

How much personal warmth is desirable? Should your managers appear aloof, inaccessible except for work-related situations, and on a last-name basis with your sales reps, or should they attempt to be one of the gang and engage in after-hours social activities with them—or something in-between?

Although this list is only partial, it illustrates the variety of behavior available to your managers. It also suggests that there is no one way to manage. Some managers' styles never seem to vary, however, because their attitudes about people (human resources) and the job (making it work) never seem to vary either. They exhibit behavior appropriate to fixing stuff. Your managers should recognize that bringing out the best in their sales reps requires them to vary their behavior, to match their behavior to the needs of their sales reps and to the demands of the situation, the context, and the desired outcomes.

THE STYLE-CLIMATE RELATIONSHIP

The relationship between style and climate can be illustrated by the situation in a large, multidivisional corporation that I observed and worked with over a number of years. Each division has its own sales force.

Division A is dominant in its market. It sells its product line to an established group of customers, all of whom are known to Division A and to its competitors. Its strategy is to maintain its market share with its current group of large customers. Servicing smaller, out-of-the-way customers is viewed as uneconomical. Because each customer can use only so much of this class of product, the sales task is to make regular and frequent "hand-holding" calls on customers, making sure that technical problems are solved quickly, adequate stocks are on hand, and customer personnel "feel good" about Division A.

As you would expect, sales reps in Division A's higher-performing districts tend to have higher needs for affiliation than do the sales reps in Division A's lower-performing districts. They seem to prefer a working climate high in support, rewards (in the form of personal approval of boss and peers), warmth, and group identity. Structure is minimal (there are few forms to fill out), and delegation and risk dimensions are low (they know where to go and exactly what to do in order to avoid losing business).

The managers in Division A's higher-performing districts do relatively little coaching in a technical sense; they prefer to accompany their sales reps on calls to help them keep the business. High standards in the form of sales quotas are absent; there's little growth in this market. The emphasis is not to lose business. Sales reps aren't encouraged to take risks, nor do they participate much in the decision-making process. On the other hand, these sales managers stress group activities (in and out of work hours), are interpersonally warm and close, take a great deal of interest in their sales reps' personal lives, and keep competitiveness to a minimum.

Division B sells its product line to contractors and is involved in maintaining contacts with architects and engineering consultants in order to get the division's product line approved for use on a myriad of individual job sites all around the country. Division B is in a highly competitive, high-growth market in which customers (contractors) come and go, opportunities to make a sale are hard to identify, and sales are hard to consummate. The sales task is highly entrepreneurial. The sales rep must discover the job site, find the contractor, get the product approved by the architects and engineers, sell the contractor, and make sure the subcontractor applies the product properly.

As you would expect, sales reps in Division B's higher-performing districts tend to have higher needs for achievement than do the sales reps in Division B's lower-performing districts (and much higher needs for achievement than Division A reps). They seem to prefer a working climate high in responsibility, risk, standards, and rewards (in the form of recognition). Structure is medium (they need help in keeping track of their commitments), and group identity is sacrificed for competitive spirit (lots of sales contests).

The managers of these higher-performing districts do a lot of coaching, particularly in the area of personal organization and time management. They set high standards, let people run their own show, encourage them to take reasonable risks, and involve them in a lot of participative, mutual decision making (the nature of the job is such that the good sales rep knows more about what's going on than the manager does). Praise is liberally dispensed as a way of ensuring recognition, but managers tend to be more socially aloof in their dealings with their people than do Division A managers. These kinds of behavior by the managers appear to foster the kind of initiative and independence this sales job requires.

The sales task in each division establishes the climate desirable for its people and product types; the manager's style should reinforce or create that climate—the way the sales reps "feel" about how to conduct the sales task. The climate tends to attract people whose needs, skills, and interests are compatible with the requirements and opportunities of the sales task. And the kind of people performing the sales task determines in large measure how well the sales tasks are performed.

THE STYLE-PERFORMANCE RELATIONSHIP

The influence of the field sales manager's behavior on task performance can be visualized by the flow shown in Figure 5.

Operationally, however, the relationship is best understood in reverse, as Figure 6 denotes.

That is, in order to know best how to behave, given a particular set of activities to manage, your managers need to understand (1) the task—what it is they are managing; (2) the need predispositions, skills, and interests of people who are most likely to perform that task well; (3) the climate variables that are most likely to produce a high-performance atmosphere; and (4) what behavior on their part is most likely to stimulate the appropriate climate perceptions.

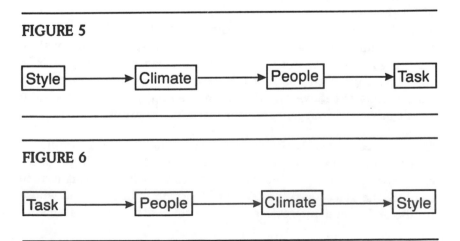

FIGURE 5

Style ⟶ Climate ⟶ People ⟶ Task

FIGURE 6

Task ⟶ People ⟶ Climate ⟶ Style

Chapter 19

Relationships

The task-people-climate-style analysis, however, is not the only determinant of how people behave as managers. In addition to working with people in groups, much of your managers' time is spent in one-on-one, or dyadic, relationships. Building and maintaining good relationships requires skill in understanding the interpersonal world.

The elements of the interpersonal world are Me, You, Us, The Situation, The Context, and The Outcome, as visualized in Figure 7.

Me is what a person brings to any given situation—values, beliefs, intellect, feelings, needs, motives, and goals. You is what the other person brings to that situation. Us is the relationship. It may be new, unfamiliar, temporary, and perhaps fraught with tension, anxiety, and suspicion. On the other hand, it may be long standing, familiar, permanent, and perhaps characterized by comfort, caring, and trust. Or it may be anywhere in between or beyond those boundaries. Me can influence You and You can influence Me. Me can influence Us and Us can influence Me. You can influence Us and Us can influence You.

FIGURE 7

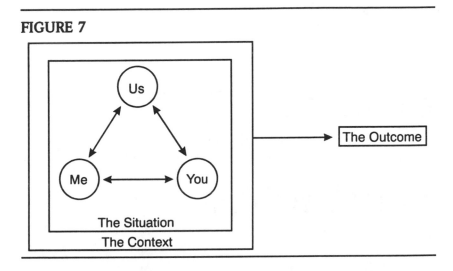

Me gives style its consistency and predictability as perceived by others. Me is heavily influenced by values, beliefs, intellect, feelings, needs, attitudes, assumptions, and expectations. A person's style contains a core of these consistent and mutually reinforcing behaviors that reflects their perceptions of themselves and their strivings toward the persons they would like to become. A certain amount of consistency in personal style is virtually guaranteed, because mentally-healthy people rarely behave in ways likely to damage their perceptions of themselves.

Whereas the general Me factors give style its consistency and predictability, specific or situational factors give style its flexibility. Much of a person's style is influenced by You—one person's attempts to respond to the needs and demands of another. People do what their boss tells them to do because it either makes sense to do it or because it seems foolish not to do it. In fact, people who have a boss (or are in contact with anyone else) whose style they admire, usually begin to emulate some of that behavior in an attempt to improve their own effectiveness.

The You factors come in all sizes and shapes. Managers respond to individual differences in other people's needs, skills, and interests in an effort to bring out the best in them while trying to maintain a high-performance climate within a heterogeneous group. People read books about management written by a You they've never met and try out the ideas in the hope that they can become more effective. They respond to the advice of a family member, a friend, or a mentor to help them cope with specific situations.

The Us factors also come in many shapes and sizes. For example, people respond to pressure from peers to conform to a set of group expectations. They respond to pressure from those who report to them in order to bring out feelings of team spirit and group loyalty. Organizations provide people with a "culture"—explicit or implicit values and ways of doing things—that define for people the key success variables in "getting ahead."

The interplay among You, Me, and Us occurs within The Situation, a combination of location, activities, and conditions at a given moment. Situations might include having dinner at home or in a restaurant, discussing a report in your office or in one of your managers' offices, playing golf, or watching a tennis match. Situations usually contain protocols—ceremonies and etiquettes that define "appropriate" behavior given the specific situation and its context.

Situation factors also determine one's style. Your managers' one-on-one behavior with their sales reps will differ from their more formal behavior toward senior management. Their negotiating styles will vary when seeking a raise from you, seeking cooperation from their peers, or seeking extra efforts from their sales reps.

Situations occur within The Context, the experience that gives the situation its meaning and purpose. The contexts of having a dinner with someone can range from romance to business; meetings in someone's office can range from a pleasant wind-down at the end of the day to an exit interview; and so on.

The Context is another determinant of style. Perceptions of increased risk or urgency in a situation may prompt your sales managers to do something themselves rather than delegate it to one of their sales reps. Perception that a particular situation may provide a sales rep with an excellent learning experience may persuade your managers to risk having a situation temporarily screwed up in order to give that sales rep a feeling of added responsibility.

Most situations have Outcomes, either positive (good) or not so positive (not so good). A positive outcome occurs when both people, Me and You, have their expectations satisfactorily met. A not-so-positive outcome occurs when one or both people fail to have their expectations met. Some situations have no outcome. This circumstance often creates "looping," in which two people end up playing the same situation over and over again.

In similar ways, the assessed outcome will determine style in a specific situation. In particular, the likelihood of a positive outcome will spur people to perform well. When people perceive that they have nothing to gain, they sink into lethargy. When they perceive that they have nothing to lose, they tend to be at their energetic, creative, happy best.

Positive outcomes are most likely to occur when the Me and the You are clear about and share a common understanding of their respective roles, their relationship, the situation, the context, and common expectations about the outcome. Not-so-positive outcomes are most likely to occur when one or more of these conditions are not met: for example, when a sales rep walks into his or her manager's office to ask a question and instead gets chewed out for a mistake made yesterday; when a trip downtown to window-shop with a spouse turns into a budget-busting shopping spree; when one person calls another by his or her first name and gets a frosty correction; or when one person asks another for advice and gets directions instead.

When Me and You get together, the sheer number and variety of possible outcomes are enormous. They might include affection, small talk, support and encouragement, praise, direction, evaluation, counseling, debate, information, help, agreement, or a sales order. And the list goes on. Many times, intuition and assessment of The Situation and The Context provide people with sufficient data regarding another person's expectations to respond appropriately. For instance, if a sales rep walks into the office of one of your

managers and asks for the phone number of the purchasing department, that information can be supplied without further ado. Often,
however, intuition and assessment fail people. For instance, if the
sales rep sticks around and starts making small talk while shifting
awkwardly from one foot to the other, that manager had better
start listening for "the agenda."

Listening improves chances for a positive outcome. It gives you the
opportunity to understand other people's definitions of their roles
and the role they want you to play, their definitions of the relationship, their understanding of the context of the situation and of the
situation itself, and their expectations of the outcome.

When your sales managers want a positive outcome, they would do
well both to listen and to assume that the other person is in a good
position to decide what to do. Unless other people expect and want
direction, information, praise or recognition, the manager's goal in
listening is to help others understand themselves better. When you
and your managers encourage other people to express and accept
differences of opinions, rather than force them to obey or agree with
you, you create conditions for high performance. The goal of listening is to help other people take responsibility for their problems
and the solutions to those problems. Effective managers seek to
develop other people's thoughts, not their own. It's another important aspect of managing motivation.

MISUNDERSTANDING

A common source of misunderstanding is role confusion. A sales
manager may at different times be a friend, supervisor, counselor,
mentor, teacher, monitor, evaluator, role model, and a source of
inspiration. Your managers should know what role they are expected to play in every situation. Sometimes people want managers
to give them a fish. Sometimes they want to be shown how to fish.
Sometimes they want to be shown where to fish. Sometimes they
just plain want to go fishing. Accurate listening can eliminate

many inappropriate responses caused by confusion about what sales reps expect from their managers and what your managers can expect from them.

Relationships are less likely to be misunderstood in work situations than in social situations—titles and organization charts being what they are. Nevertheless, have you ever experienced one of your co-workers becoming your boss? It takes a great deal of listening on everyone's part to make that transition go smoothly.

Situational and contextual misunderstandings can also be damaging. I can recall having what I thought was a pleasant lunch with one of my top sales reps. He was doing a lot of griping, but I wasn't paying much attention; he was always griping. I was keeping the conversation light—a little company gossip, the Redskins' new uniforms, mortgage rates, how his kids were doing in school, and so on. Midway through our second cup of coffee, he said, "I'm quitting."

My understanding of that situation and its context was way off-base. My pleasant lunch was his swan song. Accurate and reflective listening on my part might have prevented the loss of a good sales rep by helping both of us understand what was going on and giving both of us an opportunity for him to sort things out and perhaps reconsider.

POWER

Your managers also need to understand the relationship between power and behavior. Essentially, six sources of power are available. Two of them, physical force and coercion, we can ignore (unless you want to run your sales organization on a paramilitary basis). The remaining four, listed in increasing order of desirability for the high-performance sales force, are as follows:

Position

Sales reps acknowledge your managers' rights to command because of their titles. Relying on position to influence behavior is, however, a poor path to high performance. At best, it gains compliance; at worst, it leads to resentment and turnover among your Eagles.

Resources

Sales reps want what your managers have to give—better territories, more lucrative accounts, or special treatment. Another poor path to high performance. At best, it gains cooperation; at worst, it leads to favoritism and suggests coercion.

Information

Sales reps want to know what your managers know—a surer path to high performance than the previous two. Information sharing—teaching—leads directly to higher levels of performance and is another important ingredient in managing motivation.

Charisma

Sales reps want to be associated with your managers and what they stand for. In this respect, your managers are role models and custodians of your organization's values. When combined with information sharing, charismatic management—the ability to inspire others through personal example—is one of the most powerful external influences on your sales reps' levels of performance.

SUSPICION

Suspicion is the opposite of trust. It is endemic in most organizations. Whereas trust is fragile, suspicion is hard to root out. Whereas the conditions for trust are created over months and years, the conditions for suspicion are created in an instant, perhaps by an oversight, a slip of the tongue, or an unconscious act. The conditions for trust are hard to build and maintain. Following are accounts of some behaviors guaranteed to create problems for your managers.

Discounting

This term, borrowed from retailing, means lowering the price on a piece of merchandise. In interpersonal relationships, it means asking people to share their values, beliefs, ideas, and feelings and then indicating to them that those values, beliefs, ideas, and feelings are of little value:

> Boss: "Ben, now that you've had a chance to look over the marketing plan, what do you think of it?"

> Ben: "It looks good to me, boss. I have some reservations, however, on the pricing of the top end of the line."

> Boss: "Damn it, Ben. Who do you think you are, an economist? What the hell do you know about pricing?"

The boss can be sure from now on that she's going to hear only what Ben thinks she wants to hear. The next time she asks Ben's opinion, she's going to get only, "It looks good to me, boss." Instead of discounting Ben's opinion, the boss might have said, "You have some reservations? Let's discuss them. I'm interested in your ideas."

Finessing

A term borrowed from bridge, finessing involves setting up a situation that forces opponents to play a card they don't want to play. In interpersonal relationships, it means forcing other people to share values, beliefs, ideas, and feelings when they may not want to. The most common way to finesse someone is to make a statement in the form of a negative question:

"Don't you think holding the convention in Dallas is a great idea?"

"Wasn't the president's speech great?"

"Didn't you just love the way I fixed the roast tonight?"

How do sales reps respond to their manager if they think Dallas in August is a synonym for Hades, particularly after they complained about Palm Springs last year? How do you respond to your new next-door neighbor if you're trying hard to make friends but think the (Democrats/Republicans: pick one) have run out of good ideas? How do you respond to your spouse when you know it took three hours to prepare that roast and it tastes like the inside of a motorman's glove? Wouldn't it have been better if, in each of these instances, you just asked for their opinion instead of implying yours?

Mind Reading

This term borrowed from the gypsies, involves making inferences about another person's behavior on the basis of signs or unreliable information. The most common way to mind-read someone is to make a statement that suggests that one knows what another person is thinking:

"Alice, I gathered from the comments you made last week about working too hard that you're not interested in taking on any more new accounts. Consequently, I'm giving the United Chaos account to Sam."

This manager can be pretty sure that Alice is going to be very careful from now on about what she says around management. In fact, this manager can be pretty sure that what Alice says won't reflect what she really thinks and feels. Instead of trying to read her tea leaves, why didn't the manager say, "Alice, how do you feel about taking on another account?" and respect her ability to make the choice in this situation?

Second Guessing

This involves the substitution of one person's values for someone else's.

> "Janet, I know you deserve most of the credit for the new sales brochure. Nevertheless, we decided not to bring you along when we make the presentation to the new account in New Orleans. It will involve a lot of entertaining, and we didn't think your husband would be happy knowing you were running around all night with us guys."

Janet is not going to place much trust in people who assume that their values, beliefs, ideas, and feelings are better for Janet than her own are. (Note also the use of the managerial "we," an effort to shift responsibility to a phantom decision maker rather than a single individual.) Instead of second-guessing people, why didn't the manager say, "Janet, you deserve to play a vital part in our presentation in New Orleans. Can you make it?"

TRUST

Trust is an *attitude* that allows people to rely on, have confidence in, and feel sure about other people and things. Because trust implies the feeling that people and things won't let one down, and that situations and outcomes will occur as expected, degrees of trust are an important component of people's life stances—that set of attitudes, assumptions, and expectations people hold about themselves, other people, and the world in general. Although trust is not an observable attitude, your managers should recognize that relying, risking, and sharing does produce observable behavior.

Relying implies a free choice to commit oneself to another person. It should not be confused with *dependence,* where the choice is not free. As adults, people rely on friends; as infants, they depend on parents. To rely on one's manager requires sales reps to have confidence in their ability to predict the manager's behavior and confidence in that manager's track record to date (that is, many more positive outcomes from the relationship than negative ones). Without predictability ("I'd like to trust him, but you never know what he's going to do next"), the risks seem too great; without a satisfactory track record ("She's burned me once too often"), the rewards seem too small.

Risking implies the willingness to suffer loss in case things go wrong with the relationship. It is only when people have something to lose (money, love, security, prestige, or whatever) that the notion of trust has any meaning. The sales rep's perceived gain from trusting your managers must, therefore, be much greater than the perceived loss will be if the relationship proves untrustworthy.

Sharing implies that people give something of themselves (energy, money, time, affection, or whatever) to other people and receive something in exchange that promises a mutually desirable outcome. It's a joining of forces by sales reps and their managers to obtain something that they couldn't obtain by themselves. The mutually desirable outcome does not have to be the same for each party. Many sales reps and managers share great working relationships, with the outcome being outstanding performance by the sales rep and outstanding field coaching by the manager.

Sales reps are more likely to engage in trusting behavior when they view their managers as having *integrity* (they seem to be honest and fair in their dealings with everyone), *competence* (they seem to know what they are doing), and *openness* (they seem to have nothing to hide). Integrity, competence, and openness are qualities people assess in others that provide them with general feelings of trust in another person. In specific situations, however, even tentative feelings of trust can be enhanced by a phenomenon known as the "clarity of expectations."

This phenomenon occurs when perceptions of Me, You, Us, the Situation, and the Context are clear; when expectations of the Outcome are clear; and when all the people in the situation share the expectations. That is, in a specific situation, each person is clear about what he or she is supposed to contribute, what the other person is supposed to contribute, what the relationship is supposed to be, what protocols the situation requires, what meanings and purposes are suggested by the situation, and what the outcome of the situation is likely to be. If both sets of expectations in a specific situation are met, and particularly with regard to the outcome, a general feeling of trust between sales reps and their managers can begin to evolve.

Trusting behavior is more likely to occur in people with positive feelings about themselves and others. These people are more willing to expose themselves to the judgments of others and are more willing to rely on, take risks for, and share themselves with others. Trusting behavior is less likely in people who are pessimistic, gloomy, unfriendly, or timid.

Trusting behavior doesn't mean that one epitomizes the "sucker born every minute." Trusting behavior is subject to a great deal of differentiation. Most people exercise care in making judgments about whom to trust and in what situations. We all know people to whom we'd give the key to our safety deposit box but not tell a secret, or lend $1,000 rather than lend our car for the weekend. Because of their firm grasp on reality, people with positive feelings about themselves and others tend to be discriminating in their placement of trust. Suspicion, in the form of honest doubt, plays an important role in helping them make these discriminations.

For people with negative feelings about themselves and others, suspicion is an ever-present condition. People who feel insecure about themselves, others, and things in general tend to deny themselves the pleasure and security of trusting relationships. Suspicion, then, whether it be in the form of the honest doubt of a mentally healthy person or the generalized, paranormal response of an insecure person, must be reduced if relationships are to be characterized by relying, risking, sharing, and the realization of our expectations of positive outcomes.

Trusting behavior is evolutionary. Developing trust in others is much like developing confidence in one's self. It is a process of clarifying, testing, and working out satisfactory relationships. In the case of self-confidence, people clarify and test themselves; in the case of trust, people clarify and test others. Just as the process of developing self-confidence takes time, so does the development of trust, particularly in the testing stages. And both processes can be halted or reversed by disillusionment.

NEWTON'S LAWS

XV. What you think depends on where you sit.

Chapter 20

Activities

COACHING

Your field sales manager's most important task is to teach sales reps how to sell efficiently and effectively. Most coaching takes place one-on-one in the field; some of it takes place in small-group training sessions. Working in the field allows the manager to make calls with a sales rep and to observe, participate in, demonstrate, or take over the sale. Observation is the most common practice when making calls with sales reps. "Sidewalk critiques" give the field sales manager the opportunity to dispense praise and encouragement and to correct ineffective behavior. Participation in the sale can be an effective method of training sales reps in the finer points of such activities as answering questions, handling objections, and asking for the order. Demonstration is a tool for helping sales reps learn how to handle a module of the sale—for instance, how to make a new-product introduction. Taking over is a technique usually reserved for rescuing an important sale when it is obvious that the selling situation is beyond the sales rep's control.

High-performance sales forces are characterized by policies and practices that encourage field sales managers to spend most of their time in the field working with their sales reps (some successful companies require a minimum of 80 percent). Most of this time should be spent with Eagles. They produce most of your business; they absorb more of what your managers can teach them, which enables them to fly even higher than before; they receive direct evidence that your managers care about them and what they are doing (which reduces turnover); and they teach field sales managers things that they can bring back and share with the others.

COUNSELING

Exercising this activity requires a great deal of judgment. On the one hand, giving advice and direction in response to a sales rep's request for career guidance is an important aspect of your and your field sales managers' jobs. On the other hand, helping a sales rep or field sales manager iron out marital or financial problems is seldom wise. Your and your field sales managers cannot be expected to be priests or psychiatrists. Nevertheless, listening in a nondirective, nonjudgmental fashion to a sales rep's personal problems can be supportive and morale building when those problems influence job performance. Managers are better off confining their advice to pointing out the job-related consequences of a subordinate's personal situation, however, than becoming personally involved. The secret to effective counseling is listening.

LISTENING

To bring out the best in their people, your field sales managers have to be willing and able to listen to them. Fixit managers have difficulty listening to people. They don't see why they should and, anyway, they don't have the time. Your managers should make the time. Effective managers not only hear what other people say, they leave other people with a strong impression that they really heard what the others said and that others' thoughts and feelings are important to them. Effective managers gain understanding about other people and their needs and problems because they listen so well. They avoid making incorrect inferences from what others are saying and doing by making sure that they are listening to the reality that others are experiencing.

A person's own reality, however, makes it difficult for him or her to listen well to another person's reality. Listening well means to hear accurately what other people are saying. Hearing accurately is extracting as much meaning as possible from other people's words and from the context in which they are using those words. For instance, in response to "How are you doing?" what does "Terrible" mean? If the person has just come from the doctor's office, it could mean he needs an operation. If the person has just come from the boss's office, it could mean she didn't get a raise. If the person has just come from the ball park, it could mean that the Red Sox lost. In none of these examples does the dictionary definition convey the meaning "terrible." The attempt to extract what "terrible" means to the speaker within the speaker's own context allows the listener to distinguish among the speaker's fear, disappointment, and disillusionment.

Hearing accurately, which includes being aware of unspoken signals, is difficult because people's values, intellect, feelings, needs, and motives are unique to them and, by definition, different from other people's. These differences can produce a tendency for your managers to reject or distort what they are hearing, make value judgments about what they are hearing, and thus react inappropriately to what they are hearing.

Rejection can range from inattention ("This person is so boring I think I'll tune out") to outright blocking ("I don't like this person, so I'll ignore what I'm hearing"). Distortion can range from innocent substitution ("What they really must mean is . . .") to total misunderstanding ("But I thought you said . . .!").

Whereas rejection and distortion keep people from hearing the words others are using, the tendency to make value judgments keeps people from extracting the full meaning from other people's words. When your managers make value judgments about what their sales reps are saying, they are evaluating—approving or disapproving of what they are hearing—from their frame of reference, not the sales rep's. As a consequence, whatever subtle or not-so-subtle shades of meaning might be available to your managers if they were truly listening are lost in the busy comparison of their values, beliefs, ideas, feelings, and needs with their sales rep's.

Carl Rogers, considered the father of "nondirective counseling," identified three conditions essential to the process of listening: empathy, acceptance, and congruence. Your managers should be familiar with his notions.

Empathy is the identification with and understanding of another person's situation. Rogers goes beyond this definition to include a sense of striving to capture the quality of the feelings being expressed by the other person and attempting to experience them as if you were the other person. He argues that, in order to achieve empathy with another person, you must temporarily suspend your judgments and substitute the other person's frame of reference for yours. For most people, slipping out of their own frame of reference is incredibly difficult. For a sales rep to perceive your managers making the effort, however, is usually sufficient to improve the process of understanding. The more your managers give evidence to their sales reps that they are trying to understand the sales reps' situation and their feelings about it and that they have heard the sales reps' accurately, the more likely the sales reps are to explore with their managers the full meaning of their situations and feelings. In addition to giving managers a better picture of what their sales reps really mean, empathy also helps the sales reps understand what they themselves really mean.

Acceptance, in Rogers's parlance, includes your managers' reactions to other people as people in addition to their reactions to what other people say to them. Acceptance implies valuing others: Your managers must give a damn about people and what happens to them regardless of their behavior at the moment. Acceptance means acknowledging to people the relevance of their thoughts and feelings, as opposed to evaluating them.

Congruence is similar in meaning to the notion of authenticity. To Rogers, one person's reactions to what another person is saying must be consistent with what that person is experiencing at that moment. In other words, don't fake your responses. Whereas acceptance implies that managers are not free to evaluate, congruence implies that managers are free to express their own concern, anger, disappointment, or whatever feelings are appropriate in the context of that situation. Rogers maintains that, although congruence is difficult to achieve, if your managers' efforts to achieve empathy and acceptance are experienced by their sales reps as genuine, your managers' efforts to achieve congruence will also tend to be experienced as genuine.

Rogers's ideas suggest that one can't become a good listener (and a good manager) without really caring about people. I believe that becoming a good listener can lead to caring. People are interesting. If your managers learn to listen well—to extract as much meaning as possible from the words people use and from the contexts in which people use them—their interest in others will soon turn into caring.

REFLECTIVE LISTENING

Many professional listeners, including psychiatrists, psychologists, and certified counselors, endorse a method variously called "active listening," "responsive listening," or "reflective listening" that facilitates the process of listening for the purpose of helping someone else. I prefer the term "reflective listening," because it suggests both reflecting on and reflecting back other people's expressed thoughts and feelings.

"Reflecting on" implies total attention to the process of extracting as much meaning as possible from what other people are saying. Reflecting back implies helping other people clarify their own thoughts and feelings. In reflective listening, the listener concentrates more on the feelings being expressed than on the content of what's being said, more on the personal aspects of the situation than on the impersonal facts, more on responding to other people's agendas than on developing agendas for them.

Some helpful techniques used in reflective listening are as follows: (1) silence, appropriate when people appear to need time to consolidate their thoughts or reflect on what they have said; (2) wordless expressions such as "Mm-hm," which indicate "I'm still here and interested in what you're saying"; (3) paraphrasing, which recognizes an explicitly expressed thought or feeling—for example, "So you feel you've been mistreated?"; (4) clarifying, which attempts to spotlight an implicitly expressed thought or feeling—for example, "I take it that you're not going to let them get away with it. Am I right?"; and (5) reflecting unexpressed feelings—for example, "Wow! You really are angry, aren't you?"

Many courses and seminars are available to those who want to improve their listening skills, but while effective in helping people remember the content of what is being said, few are effective in helping people understand the nature and quality of the feelings being expressed. Fewer yet are effective in helping managers respond effectively to those feelings. The same observations can be made about books on listening. Two significant exceptions, however, are Athos and Gabarro's *Interpersonal Behavior,* which contains three excellent chapters pertaining to listening, and Rogers's *Counseling and Psychotherapy.*

Many managers have a problem with listening. They are more concerned with telling people how to "make it work" than with listening to ideas about getting things done. They are more interested in technical solutions than human problems. Listening for the purpose of helping is time consuming, and learning to listen well takes dedication, skill, and practice.

Other managers listen well, because they care. They enjoy the rewards of helping people and the challenge of trying to understand their behavior. They know that listening is the path to better understanding. And better understanding leads to better sales results. It's all part of managing motivation.

COMMUNICATION

People want to experience in other people consistency between "what they see" and "what they get." That is, a person wants another person's behavior to be consistent with what that other person values, believes, thinks, feels, and needs. This consistency is part of authenticity. Your managers would like their sales reps to behave authentically toward them—as if they have nothing to lose by sharing their thoughts with them—because if both parties can behave authentically, they can communicate well.

Good communication is the voluntary sharing of one person's thoughts with another person. It's an act of trust. Effective managers get others to share voluntarily by taking the first step. They volunteer their own thoughts first. Good communication is a manifestation of authenticity—the willingness to take overt responsibility for one's own values, beliefs, opinions, ideas, and feelings. It encourages people to dispute, explore, discuss, expand on ideas, and agree or disagree with one another. Good communication encourages understanding, for as people continue a dialogue, the disagreements that surface both "hone the razor of our intellect" and focus a spotlight on the issues. As the issues become restated and positions shift, the opportunities for consensus and commitment expand.

INSPIRING

Your field sales managers should be super-Eagles, selected for their ability to inspire Eagles to fly higher and faster. It is easier for Eagles to learn to fly higher and faster if they see that their super-Eagles are indeed super—that emulating their managers' behavior has personal and economic utility to them. The behavior your sales reps ought to be emulating is behavior that exhibits the key success factors in your business unit—the attitudes and competencies that earn people the rewards in your business unit and that enable your business unit to achieve its strategic goals. These attitudes and competencies must be embodied in your field sales managers. Furthermore, these managers need training, support, and encouragement to pass the key success factors along to their sales reps. In this way, the high-performance sales organization improves both the conformity between its sales reps' actual behavior and desired behavior, and assures that a steady stream of management talent will be available.

COUNSELING OUT

Counseling out is called for when a manager gives up on a sales rep's behavior but not on the sales rep. Sales managers who recognize a poor fit between a sales rep's talents and the requirements of the job, and little possibility to improve it, should move fast to help the person find another job that will (1) provide opportunities for him or her to grow and develop and (2) minimize the impact of his or her poor performance on the whole sales organization. For example, follow this private conversation:

> "Bill, in my professional judgment, your skills and interests aren't being given a chance to grow and develop on this job. Furthermore, this job, to be performed at the level I expect, requires different talents from ones you possess. Basically, it's a poor fit. You're a talented person, particularly good at . . .

You need a better opportunity to become the kind of person you want to become. I need a person who is better able to . . . Instead of dragging this situation on, I'd like to help you—as of right now—get your resume up-to-date, get you thinking about a better match between what you have to offer and where you best can offer it, and get you started on some interviews. How does that sound to you?"

This manager has recognized Bill's worth (specifically mentioning skills) and Bill's inability to perform (in one or more specific tasks). This manager has pointed out the poor fit, made an offer to help, including specific steps, and has checked for understanding.

Does this approach work all the time? Of course not, but it's better to try this way first than to settle for the no-win outcomes of lethargy or probation. In effective counseling out, the individual is recognized as worthy, treated with honesty, dignity, and respect, and given help in finding a potentially more productive work situation. From the organization's point of view, the opportunity to reduce rancor and ill will (all the way around), to replace a low performer with a potential high performer (without having to wait out the 90 days of probation), and to avoid the necessity of monitoring, documenting, and administering the ultimate coup-de-grace is usually well worth the effort. All it takes are managers who are competent, fair, and honest—who care about their people and take responsibility for their behavior. Some managers prefer probation in these situations. You should encourage your managers to try counseling out first because of the higher probability of a win-win outcome.

MANIPULATION

The instant infants meet the cold air, harsh light, and dry discomfort of the delivery room and begin screaming their little lungs out, they begin a life-long quest to get people to do things their way. Delicately put, we spend much of our waking lives attempting to influence other people's behavior. Less delicately put, we spend much of our lives trying to manipulate other people.

Manipulation is not a word your managers should back away from; nor should anyone else interested in the well-being of another person. Manipulation is a fact of life. It becomes "good" or "bad" only in relation to its purpose. The question is: What is the intent in manipulating another person's behavior? "Good" manipulation brings out the best in everyone involved. "Good" manipulation is when you get people to try doing something "your" way and it earns them a raise. You should encourage your field sales managers to seek behavior in themselves and others that adds value to the situation and where everyone comes out ahead—the sales rep, the manager, and other interested parties (for instance, the customer). On the other hand, "bad" manipulation produces "winners" and "losers." "Bad" manipulation is, for example, the conscious placement of a desk that preserves one person's inscrutability while casting a bright light on another person's face. Effective sales managers have nothing to hide. Nor do they play games with people's self-respect. No value is added when people's dignity is lowered by manipulative behavior that puts them down.

CONTROL

Many sales managers try to exercise too much control over their sales reps and over themselves. The former leads to suboptimal performance; the latter leads to a heart attack. When your managers exercise too much control, the performance of your sales reps tends to be equivalent to the performance of your individual managers. All you get is an additive effect; that is, at best, the whole is equal to the sum of the parts. What you really want is for the whole to be *greater than* the sum of the parts. To achieve that result, you need to hire Eagles, train them well, have your sales managers point them in the right direction, lighten up on the controls, and encourage them to fly high.

The barriers to relaxing control include pressure, training, experience, guilt, and suspicion. The pressure to achieve short-term objectives creates many situations where urgency (it's got to be done now) and risk (it's got to be done right) preclude opportunities for your managers to delegate responsibility to their sales reps. Delegation has several valuable effects on the sales reps: it tends (1) to help develop their judgment (and enrich their jobs) by giving them experience in a variety of situations and under a variety of conditions, (2) to foster creativity (they'll probably do it differently and perhaps better), and (3) to enhance their self-confidence as they learn to master new skills. You do a lot for your managers and sales reps when *you* absorb the pressure for achieving short-term objectives and keep it from influencing their behavior. You foster delegation, another effective way to manage motivation.

Past training is another barrier to relaxing control. Many managers have been taught paradigms such as management = planning + direction + control + motivation. Unfortunately, these paradigms are vast oversimplifications, and they don't work. Indeed, this one contains a serious internal inconsistency: Control tends to inhibit motivation.

Closely related to training as a barrier to relaxing control is experience. Many managers learned as sales reps how to "control the sale." Once promoted, it's a short hop from there to believing that one's job is to "control the sales reps." These managers have a short memory. As sales reps they learned pretty quickly that the customer really controlled the sale and that their success in selling came from helping their customers buy, not from trying to control their customers' behavior. Why should they think their sales reps are any different? The manager's success will come from helping the sales reps sell, not from trying to control their behavior.

Guilt and suspicion as barriers to relaxing control are interrelated. Guilt is the emotion some of your managers experience from feelings such as:

☐ "If it isn't all going smoothly and perfectly, it's all my fault."

☐ "I'm paid to get results and I don't know what's going on out there."

☐ "What's going on out there?"

☐ "Is everybody working? Is anybody working?"

☐ "Can I trust them?"

☐ "Maybe if I checked up. . . ."

It's easy for your sales managers to experience these feelings. They are paid to supervise people who are, for the most part, out of sight. If these feelings persist, the emotion of guilt will produce the attitude of suspicion. You do a lot for your managers and sales reps when you treat them with dignity and respect. In any organization, behavior tends to flow downhill.

ADMINISTRATION

Often referred to as "paperwork," administration is *not* an activity in which field sales managers should be engaged. Administration is best left to senior managers preparing for retirement, staff people (MBAs are good at it), and/or talented secretaries. The damage done by people who generate paperwork can be mitigated by restricting distribution to home-office personnel or, even better, by making generous use of paper shredders. The worst form of paperwork is the request for "information from the field." As one of my favorite sales managers puts it, "If they didn't already have the data, they wouldn't know what to ask for."

As another one of my favorite sales managers suggests, "When I get requests from the home office for information, I generally ignore them. If what they want is really important, either someone else will do it, or they'll call me back. If it's not important, it never needed to be done in the first place."

Engaging in administrative activities takes time away from what field sales managers should really be doing: coaching, counseling, listening, communicating, inspiring, and spending their time feeding their Eagles.

NEWTON'S LAWS

XVI. It's a lot easier to ask for forgiveness
than to ask for permission.

Admiral Horner

Chapter 21

Motivation

Nathaniel Branden, a psychiatrist and expert on the subject of self-esteem, has stated that no factor is more decisive in people's psychological development and motivation than the value judgments they make about themselves. He goes on to say that the nature of self-evaluation has a profound effect on a person's values, beliefs, thinking processes, feelings, needs, and goals. Self-esteem is the single most significant key to a person's behavior; thus, it is a vital concept for your managers to understand.

CHIP COLLECTING

The two components of self-esteem are lovability and capability. They are separate but related. "I am lovable" refers to feelings of self-worth—that one is worthy of existing, unconditional upon what one does, says, achieves, and so on. The first awareness of self-worth comes from the hugs, kisses, soothing noises, and other signs of affection people receive from their parents. These parental actions tell and reassure people that they are valuable, not for what they do, but for who they are. As they grow up, their circle of affection gathers more members: close relatives, playmates, friends, lovers, spouses, children, and so on. It is from this circle that people collect most of what I call *gold chips*—the smiles, touches, kind and compassionate remarks, the tender empathetic moments, the "I like you's," and "I love you's." Gold chips serve to satisfy a person's need for affection. Some gold chips are small, such as winks and shared laughter; some are huge, such as sexual activity between committed lovers. Despite the size of a particular gold chip, receiving one is evidence of personal worth and builds self-respect.

The other component of self-esteem is "I am capable." This feeling refers to self-confidence—that one has the capacity to make proper choices, take appropriate actions, and achieve desirable results. Unlike "I am lovable" feelings, "I am capable" feelings are conditional upon what a person does, says, achieves, and so on.

The first awareness of self-confidence comes from the rewards and recognitions people receive as a result of their behavior. Like signs of affection, these early rewards come from parents responding positively to infant expressions and noises. This parental behavior provides people with early encouragement to communicate, to please, to learn, and to comply. As they grow up, their opportunities for achievement widen: They earn compliments, recognition, awards, trophies. These acknowledgments of capability are what I call silver chips; they satisfy a person's need for recognition. Some silver chips are small—a sports trophy or positive remarks about a new sweater. Some silver chips are huge—winning a Nobel Prize. Despite the size of a particular silver chip, receiving one is evidence of personal capability and builds self-confidence.

Keep in mind that gold chips are unconditional rewards for being ourselves; silver chips are conditional rewards for our behavior. "I like you" is because you are you. "You look good in that sweater" is because you are wearing that sweater. Most dogs are great gold-chip dispensers. Were you to hit your dog over the head with a two-by-four, he'd still wag his tail and look at you with adoring eyes. He'd love you anyway. Most cats are great silver-chip dispensers. When you give them a good meal, they'll sit in your lap and purr. Forget them at mealtimes, and they'll raise hell. Don't feed them at all, and they'll fend for themselves.

Self-respect ("I am lovable") and self-confidence ("I am capable") work together to build self-esteem. If people don't feel good about themselves ("I'm not very lovable"), they may not take much pride in being promoted ("I don't deserve it"). By the same token, if people don't feel confident about accepting a promotion ("I'm not very capable"), they may not feel very good about themselves ("I'm in over my head").

As Branden points out, people's self-esteem is so important to them that they will do almost anything to preserve it. Furthermore, much of a person's behavior is designed to enhance self-esteem. I designed Figure 8 to illustrate the anatomy of self-esteem and its component frames of reference.

FIGURE 8

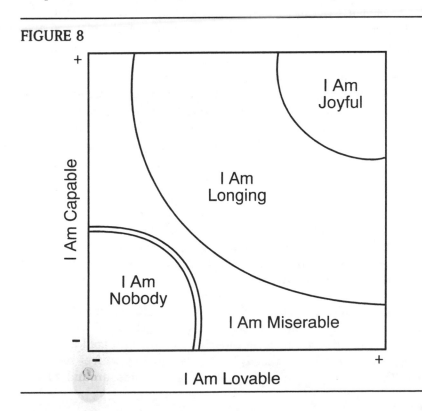

I Am Nobody: When feelings of "I'm not lovable" combine with feelings of "I'm not capable," they produce a frame of reference called "I am nobody." Although mentally healthy people may experience temporary feelings of being unworthy or incompetent, particularly in specific situations, when this frame of reference is persistent and generalized, it is paranormal at best and pathological at worst. "I am nobody" people have collected very few gold and silver chips. They feel worthless and unloved. They are potentially dangerous to themselves and to society.

Some of the common forms of behavior driven by intense "I am nobody" feelings are self-deprecation, self-deception, and self-loathing. Intense self-deprecation ("I'm no good to myself or to anybody else") can lead to various mental illnesses associated with depression. Intense self-deception ("I'm really terrific but no one appreciates me") can lead to various mental illnesses associated with losing touch with reality. Intense self-loathing ("I hate myself") can lead to extreme sociopathic behavior ("I hate everybody") and even suicide.

Fortunately, in the normal, everyday work situation (family and social situations as well), you and your managers rarely have to deal with people in the "I am nobody" frame of reference. Fortunately in the sense that such people are rare. Fortunately also because you and your managers are not equipped to deal with such people and no one should be expected to. Such people need professional help. (See Problems in Part IV.)

I Am Somebody: This classification comprises three frames of reference: "I am miserable," "I am longing," and "I am joyful." "I am miserable" is common but paranormal. "I am longing" is the state where most people are. "I am joyful" is a state where some people are and where everybody would like to be.

"I am miserable" is a better place to be than "I am nobody," but it still isn't a terrific place. It contains three groups of people. The people in the first group have collected just enough gold and silver chips to feel "barely somebody." They would like to feel more lovable, but their perception is that there's no one around to love them. They would like to feel more capable, but their perception is that there's no opportunity to make much of a difference anymore. Living and working have become a matter of going through the motions: "Nobody cares about me. Nobody cares about the work I do."

The people in the second group of "I am miserable" people have collected a lot of silver chips but very few gold ones. Everybody knows or knows of people who are achieving or have achieved the trappings of "success" but don't seem to be happy. In extreme cases, these people are the ones voted "Most Likely to Succeed" in high school, go on in college to be "All-American" and/or Phi Beta Kappa, become company president at age 40, give interviews for *Business Week*, and regularly fly to Washington on the corporate jet to testify in Senate committee hearings. But under the surface, they are desperate for gold chips. They feel unloved. They suspect their spouses of having affairs with the tennis pro. They can't remember the last time they talked to their kids. Even their dogs growl at them. Living has become a matter of achieving ever more insignificant victories.

The people in the third group have collected a lot of gold chips but very few silver ones. This group is probably smaller than the other two groups, because it is harder to feel loved without some feelings of capability. Put another way: a little love can make you forget your misery. Nevertheless, everyone knows people who are popular but not effective. They are fun to be with, but they don't get much done. And they know it. Life is passing them by.

Some of the common forms of behavior based on intense "I am miserable" feelings are driven by frustration. Some people appear to act from fear: either with great caution and timidity ("I can't afford to make a mistake") or with reckless abandon ("It can't get any worse"). Some appear to act from anger with milder forms of self-deprecation, self-deception, or self-loathing than are seen among the "I am nobody" people. Others appear to act from self-doubt: their feelings of inferiority and insecurity are expressed in arrogant behavior at one extreme and servility at the other.

Many of the people you and your managers deal with on a day-to-day basis are operating from the "I am miserable" frame of reference. Unlike the "I am nobody" people, who often resist other people's efforts to help them feel like somebody ("Anyone who likes crummy me must be crummy too"), the "I am miserable" people can be helped. This frame of reference is less stable than the "I am nobody" state.

"I am longing" is a pretty good place to be. It is where most people are most of the time. They feel pretty good about themselves. They have collected and stored sufficient silver chips to feel reasonably certain that they can solve most of their problems and take advantage of most of their opportunities. They value their accomplishments. They may long for more recognition, but they aren't desperate for it. They have collected and stored sufficient gold chips to feel reasonably important to their friends and loved ones. They value their relationships. They may long for more love and affection, but they aren't desperate for it. It is possible for them to slide back to "I am miserable," but "I am joyful" is also well within their reach. Most of the people you and your managers deal with on a day-to-day basis are operating from the "I am longing" frame of reference.

"I am joyful" is where everybody longs to be. It is usually a stable state, although grave misfortune can disturb it. Joyful people have collected and stored so many gold and silver chips that they continually have to give them away. As a consequence, they are expressive with their affection and generous with their compliments. Joyful people exude a humble self-confidence acquired by mastering a succession of situations: initiating loving relationships and maintaining strong bonds; enjoying their victories and learning from their defeats. Joyful people are enthusiastic, energetic, creative, and fun to be around. They welcome change, ignore rivalry, and take responsibility for their behavior. They enjoy life. They enjoy their work. They enjoy other people. They are authentic.

THE TRIP TO JOYFUL

Getting to joyful is a process of collecting, accumulating, and dispensing gold and silver chips. The trip begins in infancy. It can get stalled anywhere. The major roadblock is chip insufficiency caused by chip deprivation, chip refusal, or chip suspicion. Chip insufficiency is unlikely to occur if parents have gotten their children off to a good start.

Chip deprivation, withholding gold chips in particular, is common among parents who believe that giving and receiving affection is unnecessary, "unmanly," and generates vulnerability and "softness." Children raised by such parents often make good concentration-camp guards. Another form of chip deprivation is to substitute silver chips for gold ones—making children view love as a reward for good behavior: "Mommy will give you a hug if you eat all your peas." Children raised by these parents often develop abnormally high needs for achievement and end up, to use Thoreau's phrase, "leading lives of quiet desperation." Silver chip deprivation is a less common behavior among parents, but when recognition for achievement is consistently withheld from children, they can become spiritless, indifferent, and cynical.

Chip deprivation during infancy and childhood can lead to early "I am nobody" feelings, slowing the process of chip accumulation further along. One effect of early chip deprivation on adults is chip refusal: "I don't want your chip." Many people with "I am nobody" feelings view affection as seduction and recognition as exploitation. Even people with "I am somebody" feelings engage in chip refusal. In response to a compliment or an award they may say, "Just lucky, I guess." In response to "You're a nice person," they may say, "What do you mean?" Ungracious responses to proffered gold and silver chips are likely to dry up the supply.

Chip suspicion is similar to chip refusal. Instead of refusing the chip, however, these people question the motives of the chip dispenser: "I wonder what's behind all that." The chip may ultimately be accepted, albeit cut down in size by the receiver, but all too frequently it is dropped in the mud.

It seems that the lower a person's self-esteem, the harder it is for that person to collect and accumulate chips. Nevertheless, once a person gets going, chip collection—the quest for self-esteem—becomes a trip to joyful.

When chip sufficiency is achieved, generally in the "I am longing" frame of reference, chip dispensing can begin. Chip dispensing is a vital, necessary, and happy part of the trip to joyful. Although people may not have all the gold and silver chips they want, they have enough to give some away. When they do, they discover an astonishing fact: When you give a chip to somebody else, you don't deplete your own supply. It's a lot like sharing knowledge. When you tell others something they don't know, you lose nothing and they gain a lot. When people pay sincere compliments or give genuine hugs, they lose nothing and the recipients gain a lot. Indeed, when chips are graciously received, both the dispenser and receiver experience a gain in self-esteem. They both make progress on the trip to joyful.

It makes sense for you and your managers to help people make progress on the trip to joyful. When you surround yourself with joyful people, you surround yourself with people who are enthusiastic, energetic, creative, and fun to be around. Joyful people are good at getting stuff done. They make tremendous sales reps. In my terminology, they are called Eagles.

CHIP DISPENSING

You can draw one safe inference about all mentally healthy people: No matter how little you know about someone, you can assume he or she is on a quest for self-esteem. This assumption means that all mentally healthy people are engaged in the trip to joyful, and chips can help them get there. People want gold and silver chips, and they will work hard to earn them. Moreover, the trip to joyful is such that the more chips they earn, the more they want. No shred of experimental evidence exists to suggest that expressions of affection or recognition on one person's part lead to complacency on the other's. Chip dispensing then, when done under the proper conditions, is the safest and most powerful motivational tool at your and your managers' disposal.

Dispensing gold chips—whether by word or deed—is a person's way of showing affection. Because gold chips are dispensed unconditionally and not as a reward for behavior, the "I like you's," the "I love you's," the touches, the hugs, the smiles, and all the many other ways to show warmth for another person are typically expressed spontaneously. No standards of performance have to be met. No reciprocity is required. All that a person generally asks about the dispensing and receiving of gold chips is that the words and deeds be appropriate to the relationship, the situation, and the context, and that the gold chips be genuine.

In social, family, and intimate relationships, intuition and past experiences help people define appropriate and genuine behavior. In the work situation, however, affectionate behavior is normally curbed by organizational and societal expectations (unless you're in show business). Except under unusual or illicit circumstances, signs of affection are limited to responsive laughter, heartier than normal salutations, smiles, and touches. Even touching, though, can create problems. Beyond ritual handshakes, some people (many of Anglo-Saxon or Nordic heritage, for example) don't like to be touched. On the other hand, some people (many with Mediterranean heritages, for example) use an embrace to span a wide range of feelings and reactions. Between opposite-sex co-workers, when and where to touch can be a particular dilemma. As I once wrote, that hand on someone's waist is just six inches away from an ugly scene.

Acknowledging the difficulty of dispensing gold chips both appropriately and genuinely in the work situation, many people resort to dispensing *plastic chips* instead. Plastic chips have no value. They don't move another person toward joyful. On the other hand, they do little harm either. They come in several forms, the most common being "social noise" and kidding. Social noise sounds like this:

☐ "Hi! How're you doing?"

☐ "Fine, how are you?"

☐ "Good. Hot enough for you?"

☐ "Yeah. I'm about to melt."

☐ "Well, see you around"

☐ "Okay; take care."

What on earth happened? Nothing, just two people acknowledging to each other their mutual existence. Any gain? No, except perhaps the beginning of bridge building between strangers. Any harm done? No, except an opportunity is lost for one or both of them to dispense a gold or silver chip; for example, "It's really good to see you" (gold) or "That's a good-looking sweater you're wearing" (silver).

Kidding is a tentative show of affection or regard:

☐ "Did you really buy that sweater or find it in a dog kennel?"

☐ "Look who's talking. You look like you got dressed in a wind tunnel."

There's no harm done in kidding either, except, again, two people have lost an opportunity to give each other a gold or silver chip. People normally don't try to accumulate plastic chips. This variety only weighs people down on their trip to joyful. They have no motivational value. Indeed, people tend to get very tired of a kidding relationship when that's all it is, always. Occasionally, kidding makes people feel warm and close to one another. When people know that kidding is all they can expect from a relationship, however, they are unlikely to feel warm and close for long.

Praise: Dispensing silver chips—whether by word or deed—is a person's way of acknowledging another person's accomplishments and achievements. It is a key tactic in managing motivation. Unlike gold chips, silver chips are dispensed conditional upon behavior. Silver chips are the compliments, recognitions, awards, trophies, and titles people earn as a result of their behavior, whether it's a tan from a weekend at the beach or their picture on the cover of *Time* magazine. Although silver chips can be dispensed randomly or spontaneously, they are most effective when dispensed immediately following the acknowledged behavior. Indeed, the most desirable and effective way to praise another person is to dispense the silver chip in public, as soon as possible after the standards for earning the chip have been met or exceeded, and relate the chip to specific behavior.

Praise should be given in the presence of a third party (or parties) for two reasons. First, it magnifies the size of the silver chip: the larger the audience, the greater the satisfaction from the praise. Second, it endows the silver chip with validity. When your managers praise a sales rep in public, they put themselves on record and thereby give testimony to the legitimacy of that praise. The silver chip bears their seal.

Praising should be done as soon after the praiseworthy behavior occurred as possible. On-the-spot praise is the most effective. Psychologists call this action *reinforcement*. The shorter the time span between the act and the reward, the greater will be the association between the act and the reward, and thus the greater the desire to repeat the act. Sometimes conflicts arise between public praising and on-the-spot praising, as when no one is around to overhear you dispense your silver chip and you can't persuade the janitor to serve as your witness. In those kinds of situations, it's best to praise twice:

> "Sally, the way you overcame that price objection was really convincing. At the next sales meeting, I'd like you to share with the group the way you got your point across. I'm putting it on the agenda now, okay?"

Praising should be done by your managers *only* when their standards are met or exceeded. When your managers dispense silver chips for performance short of their standards, they lead their sales reps to think that because silver chips are so easy to earn, they have little value. They also lead their sales reps to think that their performance expectations are ambiguous instead of clear.

Most importantly, praising should acknowledge specific behavior. "Great job, guy; keep it up" is social noise, a plastic chip, and possibly an insincere remark. "The way you arranged your next appointment is going to save everyone a lot of time" confirms to the sales rep that the silver chip is genuine and the praise is sincere. The praise is interpreted as genuine and sincere because the sales rep *knows* that his or her actions are going to save everyone time. As public praise validates the silver chip to the recipient's outside world, specific praise confirms the silver chip within the recipient's inside world. When praising is properly done, sincerity is never an issue.

Encouragement: You and your managers should use encouragement whenever a sales rep is observed making progress toward meeting or exceeding his or her manager's expectations. Mere progress, however, does not merit dispensing a silver chip, for that behavior might lower or compromise your manager's standards. Nor does it call for dispensing a plastic chip ("Keep it up. You'll get there soon"). Effective encouragement always involves offering help. As such, it is a learning opportunity—one that increases the probability of earning a silver chip in the future. For example:

> "Your call routing is coming along nicely. Would you like me to help you get some more bugs out, or can you handle it yourself?"

To repeat, no one can get enough gold and silver chips. A person never becomes satiated with "I am lovable" and "I am capable" feelings. The more gold and silver chips people accumulate, the greater is their desire for more, and the quicker is their trip to joyful. The problem (a nice one) in dispensing silver chips is that, once you start, you must not stop. To dispense a silver chip when your expectations are met or exceeded in one instance and to with-hold a silver chip when your expectations are met or exceeded in another is behavior that, at best, confuses potential recipients and, at worst, devalues their efforts. Nothing need stop you from raising your standards and making that fact clear to others, but when people meet or exceed your standards and you don't acknowledge that fact to them, you sow the seeds of disillusionment, resentment, and feelings of "I am nobody."

Criticism: Criticism is *not* the dispensing of brown chips. *Brown chips* are the gooey, smelly, sticky, foul chips, the model for which can be found in almost any cow pasture, that some people dispense in an effort to retard or reverse other people's trips to joyful. Brown chips are the nasty, insulting, belittling, abusive, brutal verbal assaults some people use in an effort to make other people feel incapable and unlovable. Dispensing brown chips is a way of trying to turn others' "I am somebody" feelings into "I am nobody" feelings. Some managers use brown chips to try to speed things up: "Hey, dumbbell! Do it this way." Brown chips seldom speed things up; they bog things down. Effective sales managers never use brown chips, because they never use or demean people. They treat people with dignity and respect.

Effective sales managers don't criticize other *people* in order to make them feel bad. They criticize other people's *behavior* in order to help them perform better. Keeping the bad feelings from emerging (brown-chip pollution) and the learning experience from slipping away (silver-chip evaporation) requires a lot of skill and a lot of concern for other people.

Effective criticism, like effective encouragement, is characterized by providing someone with an opportunity to earn silver chips in the future. Like praise, criticism is conditional upon behavior, but in this instance, the behavior fails to meet your *minimum* acceptable standards. Again, like praise, effective criticism is related to specific behavior—but in this case, unacceptable behavior—and is given as soon as possible following the observation of that behavior. Unlike praise, effective criticism is *always* conducted in private.

Criticizing people's behavior in public can be particularly brutaliz-ing if it opens them up to ridicule or contempt. Criticizing people's behavior well after the fact calls into question the importance and significance of the transgression, as well as the motives in delaying the process. Delayed criticism produces feelings that the criticizer is trying to be vindictive, not helpful. When criticism is perceived as general rather than specific, it leads people to think that *they* are being criticized rather than *their behavior*—a sure-fire way to pro-voke defensiveness and antagonism on their part.

Finally, effective criticism is limited to unacceptable behavior. Gra-dations between marginal behavior and that which meets accept-able standards deserve encouragement: "Let me show you," "Let me help you," "Try it this way," and so on. It's easy to turn criticism into nitpicking (little brown chips) or constant cheap shots (me-dium-to-large brown chips). When people are continually criticized for marginally okay or average behavior, they tend to tune out or become discouraged, apathetic, and eventually resentful—the con-sequences of struggling out from under piles of brown chips.

Some methods are better than others for keeping brown chips from polluting the process of criticism. One such method is illustrated and analyzed here:

POLLUTION-FREE CRITICISM

Imagine a sales manager making a business call with a sales rep for the purpose of observing and coaching the latter's be-havior. Although the call itself was productive and involved no necessity for the manager to become involved, on the way into the customer's office, the sales rep apparently ignored one of the customer's key executives.

At the conclusion of the business call, the manager and the sales rep leave the customer's premises and, in the privacy of their car, the manager says: "I was really embarrassed when you walked by Sheila Henderson without saying 'Hello.' I can't tolerate behavior that appears to others to be arrogant and unthoughtful. If she were to continue to think that you exem-

plified and our company condoned that kind of behavior, it
could have serious consequences later when she takes over the
purchasing function for them. The next time, and every time
you call on them, I want you to go out of your way to see her
and talk to her. Have I made myself clear?"

Keeping in mind that the tone of the manager's voice can make this
criticism either a learning experience or an exercise in brown-chip
dispensing and assuming that the behavior on the part of the sales
rep was indeed cause for the manager to react so strongly, an
analysis of the steps in pollution-free criticism follows:

1. "I was really embarrassed" is what's known as an "I" message.
   It conveys to the listener that "I" have experienced a strong
   emotion. Because human beings tend to be drawn to one another's pain or discomfort and tend to want to nurture and
   console them, I messages tend to make a person more receptive
   to listening to what another person has to say.

2. "When you walked by Sheila Henderson without saying 'Hello'"
   is a description of a behavior, not a characterization of a person. Distinguishing between a person's behavior and the person
   responsible for that behavior is an effective way to reduce defensiveness. This objective description of the sales rep's behavior by the manager is much more likely to encourage a positive
   outcome than a subjective brown chip such as "I can't believe
   you could be so arrogant and unthoughtful as to. . . ."

3. "I can't tolerate behavior that appears to others to be arrogant
   and unthoughtful" is a clear, unambiguous description of unacceptable behavior. In other words: Don't do it anymore! Note
   the use of the first person singular: Effective managers don't
   hide behind the "royal we," the "editorial we," or the "institutional we." They take full responsibility for their behavior. Note
   also the use of "behavior that appears to others to be . . . "
   instead of "behavior that is. . . ." The former preserves the
   observer's objectivity; the latter implies a value judgment.

4. "If she were to continue to think that you exemplified and our
    company condoned that kind of behavior, it could have serious
    consequences later when she takes over the purchasing func-
    tion for them" is a statement of the consequences if this unac-
    ceptable behavior continues. It is the rationale for conducting
    the criticism in the first place. It is the justification for the
    observer's standards. Note that the consequences are related to
    shared behavior—"you exemplified and our company con-
    doned"—suggesting a shared responsibility to extricate both
    parties from this mess. This sense of shared responsibility
    paves the way for taking the following step.

5. "The next time, and every time you call on them, I want you to
    go out of your way to see and talk to her" is the most important
    step in the sequence (and the one most commonly left out, both
    in books on this subject and in actual practice). To criticize
    people's behavior without communicating to them how you
    want it done or how it can be done better is to commit the
    cheapest kind of cheap shot. Criticism is an opportunity for
    someone to learn something important and valuable. Without
    that opportunity, criticism is nothing more than a gooey,
    smelly, sticky, foul brown chip. Step 5 can be handled in a
    number of ways—for example, by telling (as in this example),
    showing, or choosing from a discussion of several options.
    Whatever method your managers use should lead to the sales
    rep's growth and development.

6. "Have I made myself clear?" is an opportunity to check for
    clarity, both of the observation and the communication, through
    the other's response. "Okay, I see your point. I'll work hard to
    develop a good relationship with her" or "I'm sorry. I was so
    preoccupied with the call that I didn't notice her. I'll apologize
    next time I see her" signal that the message probably got
    across. "Gosh, you're sure making a big deal of this. What's the
    problem?" invites further discussion and provides an opportu-
    nity to define standards and elaborate on the consequences in
    greater detail. "Hey, wait a minute! While you were in the
    restroom, Sheila and I were discussing some new product plans
    she has. I have an appointment to talk further with her on

Friday" provides an opportunity for the manager to apologize for misperceiving the situation. (Effective managers never mind apologizing when they're wrong.) Note the use of "Have I made myself clear?" instead of "Do you understand me?" The former expression acknowledges that the burden of understanding rests on the manager. The latter expression is a manager's way of testing a sales rep's IQ to see if it is sufficient to grasp the essentials of the manager's eloquent statements.

Note also that the sales manager did not mix praise and criticism (the so-called "softening blow") by saying, "You did a nice job on that call, but. . . ." This popular technique can mislead a sales rep. For one thing, it can lead to future chip suspicion, as the sales rep learns to wait for the other shoe to drop—the "but." For another, it dilutes the strength of the criticism and thus the learning experience. When your managers have to criticize someone, make sure the criticism is given once and make it stick.

NEWTON'S LAWS

XVII. People should learn from their mistakes,
not suffer for them.

Chapter 22

Managerial Growth

Your managers should be encouraged to read. Books are intellectual growth hormones. Your managers need to be well read, not only in a general-management sense but also in a liberal-arts sense. Many of the best, most relevant books for sales managers are not written for sales managers. Here is a brief list of books every manager should read. [This list also constitutes a large measure of my acknowledgements to others. Without the contributions of these authors, this book would never have appeared.]

Kenneth R. Andrews, *The Concept of Corporate Strategy* (Homewood, Ill.: Dow-Jones, Irwin, 1967). Although written primarily for a general business audience, this articulate and thoughtful book is especially valuable to marketing and sales executives.

Anthony G. Athos and John T. Gabarro, *Interpersonal Behavior* (Englewood Cliffs, N.J.: Prentice-Hall, 1978). The authors collected ideas from prominent behavioral scientists, added a number of insights of their own, and produced a highly readable, well-organized textbook for anyone interested in why people behave the way they do. The three chapters on listening are particularly well done.

Nathaniel Branden, *The Psychology of Self-Esteem* (New York: Bantam Books, 1971). For the reader interested in this subject, Branden's book goes far beyond the contents of mine. The author is a practicing psychiatrist and careful researcher, and he writes absorbing books.

Arthur W. Combs and Donald Snygg, *Individual Behavior* (New York: Harper & Bros., 1959). This book is a classic that belongs in every sales manager's library. It is readable and lively. The authors' ideas on viewing the world from the other person's point of view have influenced the thinking of many practitioners.

Karen Horney, *Neurosis and Human Growth* (New York and London: W. W. Norton, 1950). This distinguished woman is the author of several scholarly, insightful, and eminently readable books that describe why your friends behave the way they do. It's easy to become engrossed in all her books. This book is a particularly good starting point. (I have borrowed heavily from her ideas in Part IV on Unmanageables.)

Phillip Kotler, *Marketing Management,* 6th ed. (Englewood Cliffs, N.J.: Prentice Hall, 1988). This standard reference textbook for marketing belongs on every practitioner's bookshelf.

Daniel J. Levinson with Charlotte N. Darrow, Edward B. Klein, Maria H. Levinson, and Braxton McKee, *The Seasons of a Man's Life* (New York: Alfred A. Knopf, 1978). Reading this book can be an extraordinary experience. The insights gathered and presented are the foundation for a compelling theory of adult development. The content of this book, which includes case histories, makes it almost impossible to put down. (I have borrowed heavily from these ideas in Part IV on the adult life cycle.)

George H. Litwin and Robert A. Stringer, Jr., *Motivation and Organizational Climate* (Cambridge, Mass.: Division of Research, Harvard Business School, 1968). A good compilation of the authors' work and the contributions of others in the development of the concept and utility of organizational climate. See also, from the same publisher, *Organizational Climate,* Renato Taguiri and George H. Litwin (eds.), 1968.

Douglas McGregor, *The Human Side of Enterprise* (New York: McGraw-Hill, 1960). If I were beginning to build a library of high-performance management books, this book would be the first one I'd buy. It's all about Theory X and Theory Y.

Carl R. Rogers, *Counseling and Psychotherapy* (Boston: Houghton Mifflin, 1942). Despite its forbidding title, this book is interesting, easy to read, and highly relevant to sales managers. The author is widely recognized as the expert on listening, and this book articulates his theories and techniques well.

Carl R. Rogers, *On Becoming a Person* (Houghton Mifflin, 1961). The author's widely accepted views on the process of self-actualization are interestingly presented here. Another "must" book for the sales manager.

Philip Selznick, *Leadership in Administration* (Evanston, Ill.: Row Peterson and Company, 1957). This book is not easy to read, but it packs more insight about and understanding of leadership in 154 pages than you can find anywhere else. If you want a book you will read and reread and from which you will gain greater rewards with each reading, get your hands on a copy of this one.

Richard M. Steers and Lyman W. Porter (eds.), *Motivation and Work Behavior* (New York: McGraw-Hill, 1975). Another good collection of articles by and about the motivational theorists, this book is broader in coverage than the Vroom and Deci book listed next. Both books, however, appeal primarily to the serious student of management.

Victor H. Vroom and Edward L. Deci (eds.), *Management and Motivation* (New York: Penguin, 1970). This good collection of articles written by the best known motivational theorists, including Maslow and Herzberg.

And anything written by Peter Drucker!

PROFESSIONAL BEHAVIOR

Managerial growth requires responding to change and diversity. The Me changes as one grows and develops. The You changes as one's life crosses the paths of others who are growing and developing, too. The Us changes as relationships are formed and unformed. The Situation, The Context, and The Outcome change as people move, get transferred, get promoted, or otherwise change their life styles. Some of these changes are rapid, even kaleidoscopic in their ability to produce chaos and stress in a person's life. Other changes are gradual, almost imperceptible, and easily taken in stride. Whether the changes are rapid or gradual, significant or inconsequential, traumatic or tranquil, your managers have a choice: Their responses can be random or they can be professional.

A lot of young people say "I want to do my own thing" in one breath and "I want to be a manager" in the next. That's one particular cake people can't have and eat too. People give up their right to do their own thing when they take on the responsibility for someone else's work-related behavior.

Random behavior is "doing my own thing." It's inappropriate when another person's welfare is at stake. Random behavior is characterized by a focus on Me to the exclusion of the realities of You, Us, The Situation, The Context, and The Outcome. It is characterized by an inadequate understanding of the managerial or selling tasks; the needs, skills, and interests of the people involved; the climate variables most likely to encourage high levels of performance and job satisfaction; and the managerial behavior required to stimulate accurate perceptions of that climate.

Professional behavior is marked by caring and by treating others with dignity and respect. Professional behavior embraces the attitudes and skills required to deal with the realities of You, Us, The Situation, The Context, and The Outcome, while maintaining the integrity of Me. These notions also provide your managers with the analytical power, discipline, and patience to work effectively with the task-people-climate-style relationship.

Professional behavior is as follows:

☐ having an active concern about the life, growth, and needs of other people

☐ taking the time to assess and measure the impact of one's words and deeds on other people

☐ taking personal risks on another's behalf

☐ ensuring that people learn from their mistakes, not suffer for them

☐ helping people choose behavior that leads to their growth and development

☐ encouraging people to fly high, fly free

☐ giving credit, not taking it

☐ helping people bring out the best in themselves

☐ being sensitive to people's situations in life

☐ providing people with tools to make better decisions

Although adaptability—a person's capacity to respond to changing circumstances—is a hallmark of the professional manager, some people are disturbed by the idea that professionalism will produce or stimulate behavior that is too adaptable—that to be effective, managers have to become chameleons and take on too many "disguises," or that they must become so flexible they lose their backbones. Enough Me exists in professional managers, however, to keep them from losing their identities. Core values lend a measure of consistency and predictability to professional managers so they continue to behave like authentic people.

Some managers appear rigid, inflexible, dogmatic, and impatient. They enjoy fixing stuff, and about the only responsiveness they need to show is when they are faced with something they've never had to fix before. Even then, give fixit managers enough time, enough tools, and enough people to blame, and they'll get the stuff fixed—which proves to them that it pays to be rigid, inflexible, dogmatic, and impatient. Your managers should anticipate change. They should realize that to get new things done involves doing things differently—responding to new tasks, new people, and new workplace climates, and initiating new behavior on their part.

It is essential for your field sales managers to exhibit professional behavior. If they don't give a damn about their sales reps, their sales reps won't give a damn about them. And the trip to lethargy will begin.

Caring for others is not the same as "being soft on" people. Effective sales managers do not appear one-dimensionally at some point on a continuum between kissy-face management and MBA (Master of Brutal Action) management. Nor do they appear two-dimensionally as a point on a grid with "people-oriented" as one axis and "results-oriented" as the other. Effective sales managers are three-dimensional people whose caring for others make them capable of a variety of effective behaviors in a variety of circumstances. The Eagles and others your managers must care for are the subject of Part IV.

NEWTON'S LAWS

XVIII. Toughness and gentleness
are not mutually exclusive traits.

PART IV

THE PEOPLE:
EAGLES AND OTHERS

Chapter 23

Theories

One clear distinction that can be made between sales managers is that some try to *prevent negative* work attitudes among people, whereas others try to *foster positive* work attitudes. The former group of managers concentrates on working conditions, salary increases, and carrying out "policy." The latter group concentrates on recognizing people's accomplishments and achievements, and providing them with opportunities for personal growth and development.

The former activity is a lot easier than the latter. When dispensing silver chips, your managers can assume that everyone aspires to higher levels of self-esteem. What constitutes the personal growth for one person, however, is not the same for another. Sales reps are individuals, each with different sets of needs and aspirations, and each with different sets of values, beliefs, attitudes and feelings. When your managers attempt go beyond chip dispensing and satisfying their sales reps' most basic job needs, they find that other needs and aspirations are hard to recognize and thus hard to satisfy. For one thing, few people truly understand why they behave as they do. For another, few people are comfortable sharing their needs, aspirations, and motives with another (particularly their boss!).

Although your managers are totally responsible for their own behavior and all the forces that influence that behavior, the quandary for people such as your managers (and also parents, teachers, and so on, who take on temporary responsibility for the behavior of other people) is that they can't be held responsible for the forces that influence other people's behavior. Nor can they be held responsible for understanding people.

Short of becoming a psychiatrist—which your managers are not expected, trained, or paid to be—the only safe way out of this quandary for your managers is to discipline themselves to deal with other people's *behavior,* not with other *people.* Your managers have the obligation and responsibility to try to modify the behavior of their people; they have no right to try to modify their people.

For example, your sales managers are not paid to make people more conscientious or improve other aspects of their "attitude." They are paid to influence sales reps to make better sales calls. When your managers are successful in modifying a sales rep's behavior, they may make some impact on the sales rep's attitude, but the nature and quality of that impact is beyond your managers' control. The nature and quality of that impact is the responsibility of the sales rep. If someone has an "attitude" problem, that's for a psychiatrist to handle. If someone has a problem making cold calls, that's for your managers to handle. Nevertheless, in order to manage motivation you and your sales managers should be familiar with the prominent theorists and their ideas about why people behave the way they do. Keep in mind that these ideas are theories and that your managers aren't psychiatrists. Encourage your managers to avoid "playing shrink."

HERZBERG

An interesting and useful insight into motivation is Frederick Herzberg's Motivation-Hygiene theory. His research uncovered five factors associated with job satisfaction: achievement, recognition of accomplishment, the work itself, responsibility, and advancement. He called these factors "satisfiers." He also identified six factors associated with job dissatisfaction: company policy and administration, supervision, salary, interpersonal relations, and working conditions. He called these factors, "dissatisfiers."

Herzberg suggested that satisfiers and dissatisfiers have different focuses: satisfiers relate to what a person does (are intrinsic); dissatisfiers relate to the situation in which the person does it (are extrinsic). Furthermore, satisfiers are motivational factors that have a positive effect on work attitudes; dissatisfiers are hygiene factors that work only to prevent a negative work attitude. Herzberg maintains that needs do not necessarily exist on a continuum between high and low motivators; they may exist on separate continua. That is, the opposite of job satisfaction is not job dissatisfaction but no job satisfaction. The opposite of job dissatisfaction is not job satisfaction, but no job dissatisfaction. Motivators turn people on; hygiene factors keep people from turning off.

A motivator, such as recognition for a job well done, provides people with more incentive to perform well than does a hygiene factor, such as the prospect of a salary increase. Similarly, a negative hygiene factor, such as difficulty getting along with the boss, provokes more disinterest in work than a negative motivator, such as a failure to earn a promotion. Herzberg suggests that motivators contribute to human growth and development; hygiene factors enable people to avoid unpleasantness.

Your managers should be sensitive to the distinction between intrinsic motivational factors and extrinsic hygiene factors. Each makes a separate, distinctive contribution to high performance. Some managers concentrate their efforts on preventing negative work attitudes. They think they are motivating people when they are nice to them and provide them with a fancy title, a nice office, and a big bonus at Christmas. If they are smart, managers soon learn that these actions aren't enough, that "Money can't buy you love." Your managers should work hard to minimize job dissatisfaction, but they should also focus on going beyond hygiene factors to provide their people with challenge, recognition, and opportunities for growth and development.

MASLOW

Abraham Maslow created a popularly recognized theory of motivation called the Hierarchy of Needs that sheds light on people's needs and how they satisfy them. Your managers should be familiar with this classic theory. People's needs add purpose to their behavior. Some needs are required, such as air to breathe; some are wanted, such as a promotion. Once a person becomes aware of a need and identifies it, that need becomes a motive, the source of that person's goal-directed behavior. When managers refer to another person as "motivated," they are describing a person experiencing a need that is being (or is about to be) converted into behavior.

Maslow pointed out that a need once satisfied is no longer a motive. Hunger may cause people to salivate at the sight and smell of a hamburger. Once that appetite is satisfied, however, the sight and smell of another hamburger is unlikely to have much impact on them.

Maslow categorized needs based on a hierarchy that determined the order in which a person's needs have to be satisfied. His hierarchy can be conceptualized as shown in Figure 9.

FIGURE 9

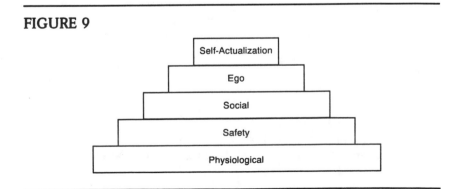

The most basic needs are physiological—such things as food, sleep, water, warmth, and air. If people are deprived of sufficient amounts of a physiological need, their behavior is dominated by it. On the other hand, the adequate satisfaction of these needs is unlikely to alter their behavior much at all. People ordinarily barely notice breathing, but their behavior becomes frantic when they lose track of their mouthpiece while scuba diving. People normally pay little attention to toilets. They will risk missing a plane, however, if their bladders become sufficiently distended.

Given the adequate satisfaction of physiological needs, the next set of needs that requires satisfaction is, to use Maslow's terminology, safety needs. Because society provides people with a relatively orderly and predictable environment, safety needs rarely dominate people's behavior as much as physiological needs. Nevertheless, the need to be free from the threat or actuality of physical harm, disease, and natural and human-made catastrophes can produce a variety of significant behaviors when a person feels endangered. And, when the threat is lifted, just as when hunger is satisfied by the hamburger, so is fear abated. When people learn that their company's "downsizing" plans do not include them, they relax.

Once safety needs are fairly well satisfied, Maslow considered social needs as emerging preeminent. These needs are people's desires for love, affection, and belonging. When people are deprived of the company of family, friends, co-workers, or the company of people in general, they will take strong measures to provide themselves with relief from feelings of ostracism, loneliness, and emotional deprivation.

The next motivators Maslow identified are ego needs. People need to feel good about themselves, who they are, what they do, and how well they do it. Maslow further classified ego needs into internal (desires for self-confidence, independence, and freedom) and external (desires for respect, recognition, and appreciation). Deprivation of these needs, Maslow pointed out, leads to feelings of inferiority and helplessness.

Even when physiological, safety, social, and ego needs are met, people may still not be satisfied. Maslow identified the need for self-actualization as the ultimate motivator. Self-actualization, as Maslow defined it, is more than the army recruiting slogan, "Be all that you can be." It is "Becoming everything that one is capable of becoming." Complete actualization is doing what we are fitted for. In Maslow's words, it is "What you can be you must be." Maslow distinguishes physiological and safety needs as "lower-order" needs and social, ego, and self-actualization needs as "higher-order" needs.

Maslow's theory has received wide acceptance, particularly in management circles. It is intuitively obvious (indeed, the theory seems so "right" that, to my knowledge, it has never received experimental verification). Particularly obvious is the order of needs: the desire to make of oneself what one can requires a positive feeling about oneself, positive feelings of affection from others, a strong sense of physical and emotional safety, and the maintenance of one's physical being.

It is also useful. In Maslow's words, "Man is a perpetually wanting animal." Thus, sales managers who help their people achieve the satisfaction of their needs—in particular their higher-order needs—are in a much better position to provide their people with powerful motives to perform well than are managers who concentrate only on physiological and safety need satisfaction: the paycheck.

McCLELLAND

Although people tend to share the same needs and to experience similar motives, most people vary in the strength of their needs. This variability is an integral part of people's frames of reference and drives much of what people think about, prefer doing, and do well. David McClelland has studied three of these motives extensively: the needs for achievement, affiliation, and power. (I introduced these ideas of his in the discussion of Climate Variables in

Part III.) He calls these three "social motives," because they are such powerful influences on interpersonal behavior. Although all people experience these needs, it is the degree to which one motive predominates that predisposes a particular individual to behave in a particular way.

People with a high need for achievement gain their primary satisfaction from setting goals for themselves and striving to meet these goals. Setting moderate goals is best, because if the goals are too low, these people find no satisfaction in meeting them; if they're established too high, there is the possibility of too much frustration. Such people enjoy accomplishing things, building things, and solving problems. They tend to be competitive. They enjoy taking responsibility for their actions. The risks they take are calculated. They prefer games of skill to games of chance. They need constant feedback on how well they are doing. They enjoy having their results measured. They spend a lot of time thinking about how they are going to do things and how things can be done better. Alexander Horniman, a colleague of mine, calls them the "Be Perfect" people.

People with a high need for affiliation gain their primary satisfaction from establishing and maintaining relationships with other people. Liking and being liked are very important to them. They prefer to be with other people rather than be alone. They enjoy parties; they excel at small talk; and they prefer to work within warm, friendly, cohesive groups. They exude team spirit and value compassion and camaraderie. They tend to be less concerned about how well they are doing than about what others think of them. They spend a lot of time thinking about the feelings and concerns of others. They are Horniman's "Be Nice" people.

People with a high need for power gain their primary satisfaction from being able to gain influence over other people. They enjoy controlling events and situations. They enjoy organizing things. They value efficiency and showing others how to do it "right." They seek the status and activities of leadership. McClelland points out that the need for power, in a negative sense, can lead to dominance, personal "win-lose" situations, and "the law of the jungle." In a positive sense, it can lead to exercising influence on group achievement, such as in joining and leading charitable, social, or political organizations. These people are Horniman's "Be Strong" people.

These three need categories predispose people to behave in more or less predictable ways. But they don't guarantee it. Indeed, making inferences about someone else's needs can lead to inaccurate conclusions. Nevertheless, people's needs have an important bearing on their interests and skills. People with *extraordinarily* high needs for achievement may feel frustrated working on projects with long time horizons but may be challenged by working on projects involving the achievement of a series of short-run objectives. People with *extraordinarily* high needs for affiliation may feel frustrated working by themselves but may feel fulfilled by working on projects requiring a lot of teamwork. And people with *extraordinarily* high needs for power probably won't enjoy jobs that have little opportunity to influence others, but they may excel in positions that allow them to advise, manage, and teach.

Certain psychological tests can uncover these need predispositions in people. It's unnecessary to go that far, however. Skilled interviewing can usually uncover what you need to know. Sales tasks that entail frequent opportunities to make a sale, sometimes called "transactional" selling, will appeal to people with high needs for achievement. Sales tasks that involve building relationships with groups of people, internal and external, all of whose members are involved in consummating the sale, sometimes called "relationship" selling, will appeal to people with high needs for affiliation. Sales tasks that require coordination and management of complex situations and activities to make a sale, sometimes called "executive" selling, will appeal to people with high needs for power.

McGREGOR

In Maslow's terms, people work to earn the wherewithal to satisfy their physiological and safety needs: to feed, clothe, shelter, protect, educate, and generally provide for themselves and their families. According to Maslow, they also work

☐ to earn the affection of friends and loved ones and for the sense of affiliation and belonging that comes from accomplishing tasks with other people

☐ to maintain and bolster their self-esteem—to reinforce feelings that their activities are worthy of them and that they perform these activities well

☐ because work is an important part, not only of their being, but also of their becoming—a vital element in self-actualization: the quest to become everything that we are capable of becoming

In Herzberg's terms, people work

☐ to achieve

☐ to gain recognition for accomplishments

☐ to enjoy the work itself

☐ to feel responsible for their actions

☐ to advance in influence and life style

☐ to avoid dissatisfaction and deprivation

In McClelland's terms, work is a way of satisfying needs for achievement, affiliation, and power. These three theorists all suggest that, once our physiological and safety needs are met, our motives for working center on the satisfaction of higher needs relating to self-confidence, self-worth, and self-actualization.

No one has collectively captured these ideas better than Douglas McGregor, the creator of Theory X and Theory Y. The set of assumptions about human nature in Theory X is that, in order to get work done, people need to be persuaded, rewarded, punished, controlled, and directed by others. The foundation for this set of assumptions is the belief that people are naturally lazy and self-centered, lack ambition, dislike responsibility, prefer to be led, resist change, and are not very bright. The behavior by individual managers that corresponds to these assumptions and beliefs is to organize, direct, monitor, and control people's actions in order to match their behavior with the needs of the organization. This behavior is commonly referred to as "carrot and stick" management.

The behavior of organizations that corresponds to Theory X assumptions and beliefs focuses on attempts to satisfy people's physiological and safety needs. They pay good wages and offer generous fringe benefits, secure employment, and good working conditions. Why, then, they ask, don't people work harder? Remember Maslow: A satisfied need is no longer a motivator. People want more out of work than extrinsic satisfactions. Work is an opportunity to satisfy higher-level needs. Organizations that concentrate their financial and managerial resources on lower-level need satisfaction may deprive their members of adequate satisfaction for their higher-level (social, ego, and self-fulfillment) needs. To quote McGregor, "Man lives by bread alone when there is no bread." When people in an organization are deprived of opportunities for growth and development, your managers receive passivity, resistance to change, and demands for more bread.

McGregor proposed a new set of assumptions about human nature and called it Theory Y. It assumes that, in his words, "the motivation, potential for development, capacity for assuming responsibility, and the readiness to direct their behavior towards organizational goals are present in all people." The foundation for this set of assumptions is the belief that people are *not* lazy and passive; they become so only when their work deprives them of the opportunity to achieve their social, ego, and self-fulfillment goals. The managerial behavior that corresponds to these assumptions and beliefs provides people with working conditions that encourage them in their efforts to grow and develop by helping them direct their own efforts toward the needs of the organization. The behavior of organizations that corresponds to Theory Y assumptions and beliefs involves, quoting McGregor again, "creating opportunities, releasing potential, removing obstacles, encouraging growth, [and] providing guidance."

McGregor was quick to point out that Theory Y is not "soft" management, an abrogation of a manager's responsibility to get results. Rather, it is a way of thinking about how to get results by getting the best out of people—namely, by unlocking the potential within them.

SELF-ACTUALIZATION

Some managers tend to view people as "human resources," as useful components for helping them fix stuff, as static bundles of skill and energy deployed for the purpose of achieving organizational ends. A better approach for your managers is to view people as individuals—with individual needs to grow and develop, with unique views of themselves and of who they want to become. This approach creates the conditions that help people become the kinds of people they want to become.

In addition to self-esteem—the group of perceptions that define for people the value they place on themselves—people also hold a group of perceptions that define for them who they are. Various writers call these definitions the "self-concept," "self-image," or "actual self." I prefer to use "actual self" in this book, keeping in mind that the way people perceive and describe themselves may not agree with how other people perceive and describe them.

The actual self is a broader frame of reference than self-esteem. It has many other facets. It includes all the roles people play and the degree of skill they exhibit in playing those roles, for instance: "I am a devoted parent who spends a lot of time with my children, teaching them and playing with them. I am a good spouse who loves and respects my marital partner, provides well for my family, and exhibits a talent for resolving conflicts. I am loyal to my friends, willing to give them the 'shirt off my back.' I am a dependable employee who works a little harder than I need to in order to avoid letting anyone down. I am a pretty good manager, although I wish I could exhibit more patience when listening to my subordinates. I am usually the life of the party, a very good joke-teller. I am a lousy tennis player."

It also includes all the characteristics, qualities, and attributes, both positive and negative, that people acknowledge they possess, for instance: "I am trustworthy, honest, capable of keeping secrets, friendly, and funny. But I can also be moody, short-tempered, and impatient. I am careful about how I spend my time but careless when it comes to spending money. Basically, I am lazy."

The actual self also includes the titles, formal descriptions, and identifications with groups that people use to describe themselves—for instance: "I am a college graduate," "I am married," "I am a sales manager," "I am a female Caucasian," "I am twenty-seven," "I am a Rotarian," "I am a Roman Catholic."

These examples are necessarily brief and restricted; obviously, people can describe themselves in an almost infinite number of ways and play myriad roles. (An interesting experiment: write a one-page description about yourself. Ask several friends, co-workers, or employees to write a one-page description of you. Compare the write-ups. Usually, self-descriptions made by mentally healthy people will match quite closely with other people's descriptions of them.)

The actual self is dynamic; its component parts vary in strength and importance. Although the actual self is derived from past perceptions and the value judgments people make about them, new perceptions make changes in the way people see themselves, including changes in their actual selves. People gather new evidence about themselves all the time, and as with any other perceptions, people accept, modify, distort, or reject them depending on the circumstances at that moment.

Component parts of the actual self vary in stability and resistance to change. Some of the roles, attributes, and titles people include as part of their actual selves are easily modified, either because the perceptual evidence that causes a change is incontrovertible (a divorce or a promotion, for example) or because the role, attribute, or title is a relatively peripheral part of their actual selves ("I thought I was a pretty good bridge player until I sat down with these folks"). Some facets of the actual self are so central, however, that people will do anything, including rejecting or distorting perceptual evidence, to avoid damage to those facets. Take, for example, the "perfect" parents who reject the teacher's advice to ease up on their children, or the aging "tennis champions" who blame the pounding in their chests on the humidity instead of their cholesterol levels. If being a perfect parent, an outstanding athlete, or anything else for that matter is central to a person's actual self, nothing short of a major trauma, such as a drug-dependent child or a heart attack, will modify that facet of the person's actual self. Sometimes even traumas won't do it.

As a result of the importance people place on their actual selves, much of their behavior is driven by the need to maintain and enhance it. They spend time with their children, surprise their spouses with flowers, and treat their friends to an unexpected "this one's on me," not only because these acts give them pleasure, but because the acts maintain their positive feelings about themselves as parents, spouses, friends, and so on.

People also act to enhance their actual selves by striving to become their ideal selves—better parents, spouses, friends, and so on—and by striving to reduce the negative feelings they have about themselves. Whereas the actual self is a group of perceptions people hold that define for them who they are, the ideal self is a group of expectations people hold that define for them who they want to become. As with the actual self, the ideal self also has many facets: ideal parent, ideal spouse, ideal friend, ideal lover, ideal tennis player, and so on.

Self-actualization is a term used to describe the continuous striving to close the gap between people's perceptions of the persons they

are—their actual selves—and the persons they want to become—
their ideal selves. Closing the gap, to use Maslow's words again, is
"becoming everything that one is capable of becoming."

As mentally healthy people grow older and more mature, their
definitions of themselves—actual selves—become more accurate,
that is, more consistent with the ways other people define them.
People learn (sometimes the hard way) more and more about themselves and what they can and cannot do. These data come from
their successes and mistakes, triumphs and disasters, gold chips
and silver chips, self-judgments and the judgments of other people.
These experiences allow mentally healthy people to modify their
actual selves, making them more "real." Mentally healthy people
are also capable of modifying their ideal selves. And as they grow
older and time begins to slip away, experience tempers their notions of who they can become and what they can achieve.

These modifications in the actual and ideal selves make up a large
part of what people call "wisdom." At first glance, age and maturity
appear to close the gap between actual and real. For some people,
this is true. For others, however, age and maturity bring new definitions of actual self and ideal self that maintain the process of
self-actualization throughout their lives.

Some managers view the motivations of people as seeking comfort
and attempting to preserve the status quo. This attitude is typical
of Theory X. Other managers view people as pursuing self-actualization and assume that this activity is a powerful force in influencing people's behavior, whatever their age. These managers, whose
attitudes are typical of Theory Y, attempt to create the conditions
wherein people can grow and develop. When the organization's
goals are perceived by people as helping them become their ideal
selves, the process of self-actualization for individuals can lead to
high performance for the organization.

Note the similarities among people engaged in healthy, productive
self-actualization and the people described previously as authentic
and joyful. *Self-actualization* is a process of becoming everything

people are capable of becoming, of closing the gap between the reality of who they are and realistic models of who they want to become. Authentic people perceive their world and themselves realistically. They take full responsibility for their own behavior. They take delight in the experience of other people's uniqueness. As a consequence, they relate effectively to other people. Joyful people exude a humble self-confidence gained from mastering a succession of situations. They are enthusiastic, energetic, creative, and fun to be around. They welcome change, ignore rivalry, enjoy life, enjoy their work, and enjoy other people. Eagles tend to be authentic, joyful, and busily engaged in healthy, productive self-actualization.

REALITY

Obviously, money is an important motivator, but it is easy to make incorrect inferences about its importance to another person. At the physiological and safety levels, money is a critical and necessary factor: Too little of it causes physical and emotional deprivation. But at the social, ego, and self-actualization levels, money loses much of its power to motivate people. For example, many studies have shown that people will voluntarily reduce their output, and thus their earnings, in order to maintain good relationships with their co-workers. Many people, such as teachers and nurses, suboptimize their incomes for other benefits they derive from their work. Other people turn down promotions and transfers in order to keep their children in familiar schools.

At the higher need levels, however, money may take on a more symbolic quality. People desire to earn more of and are willing to work harder for what money stands for: power, achievement, status, and "success." For many people, their salary level is their scoreboard in life—a tangible measure of their worth to themselves and to society.

Your managers should not ignore the power of money to influence behavior, but they should also not rely on the compensation plan to do their motivating for them. Money is but one element in managing motivation. Effective sales managers are especially sensitive to the needs, desires, and strivings of others. They should strive to understand what money represents to each of their sales reps when they attempt to influence the sales rep's behavior. Some sales reps (even some of your Eagles) would rather take an occasional Wednesday afternoon to play golf than increase their annual earnings by ten grand.

Experiences within people's working life, as so many writers have shown, have the potential to satisfy many of their higher-level social, self-esteem, and self-actualization needs. Work experiences can range from the camaraderie of the company bowling team to the shared responsibilities of the corporate boardroom, from a slap on the back for a job well done to a six-figure bonus for turning around an unprofitable division, from solving a simple assembly problem to creating a whole new manufacturing procedure. Experiences within the working life also have the potential to provide people with the gold and silver chips that make them feel better about themselves and the work they do. As people acquire and develop new skills, they can become more self-assured; as they gain experience working with others, they can become more trusting; as they achieve recognition, they can become more optimistic.

Before getting carried away by the notion that work can be some sort of self-development heaven or an inexhaustible fountain of higher-order need satisfaction, your managers should recognize that for too many people work is a grind, a boring routine necessary to avoid starvation or welfare, or a way out of the particular hell in which they find themselves. It is extremely difficult for people consumed by the need to make it past the poverty level to be much concerned about whether their work is fulfilling or not. The silver chips they need have portraits of George Washington engraved on one side and "United States of America" on the other.

Nevertheless, recalling Herzberg's idea that hygiene factors are unlikely in themselves to foster individual growth and development, effective managers try to create conditions whereby everyone has the opportunity to pursue whatever *work-related* goals are paramount to them at that point in their lives. They recognize that the attempt to close the gap between the actual self and the ideal self is one of the strongest motivators behind the behavior of mentally healthy people. Both compassion and common sense dictate that, even in the most menial work activities, job content should include some elements of initiative, responsibility, and ingenuity. For without the *opportunity* for growth in these areas, people at work become robots—apathetic at best, resentful at worst. Although few people consider sales reps to be performing menial work, your managers should be acutely aware that their sales reps need to be offered a great deal of opportunity for personal growth and development, or they'll become robots, too.

NEWTON'S LAWS

XIX. Some people sit on their hands
because there's no place else to sit.

Chapter 24

Problems

In the ideal world, sales organizations create the holes to fit the pegs, and sales managers hire people and find useful and creative things for them to do. In the real world, sales organizations need pegs to fit specific holes, and sales managers hire people who can be fitted into these holes.

A poor peg-hole fit produces turkeys, people who evidence poor performance and low job satisfaction. Effective managers are quick to recognize turkeys: the skills and aptitudes are inappropriate; the interests aren't there; the attitudes aren't productive; and the needs of neither the organization nor the individual are being satisfied.

When the requirements of the hole can't be modified to fit the needs of the peg—the all too frequent reality of organizational life—managers are faced with several options. One is to "work with" the turkey. Although nature converts caterpillars into butterflies, rarely can your managers convert a turkey into an Eagle. Nor should they try. Time spent on this low-probability effort is better spent on feeding Eagles. Furthermore, to keep turkeys hanging around deprives them of the opportunity to become Eagles in some other job in which their skills, aptitudes, interests, and attitudes are better suited. A better option than working with turkeys is prompt counseling out. If this action isn't taken, the no-win situations of learned helplessness, probation, and/or termination will occur.

Learned Helplessness

Learned helplessness occurs when both the individual and the manager (acting for the organization) give up, for example:

> "Good ole George is a nice guy but he's a real clunker. He'll never amount to anything in sales. But we hired him, so I guess we gotta keep him around."

Why will George "never amount to anything" and why do "we gotta keep him around"? Why do people give up?

When confronting an event that has an outcome potentially important to them (for example, "This could be a big sale"), if people perceive that they have a good deal of control over that outcome (such as "Right now, I've got the inside track") they are likely to expend a lot of effort in pursuit of that outcome. On the other hand, when people believe that their response to a situation will not be related to the eventual outcome—that they have no effect on the situation or control over the outcome—or that the outcome is inconsequential to them, their desire to influence the situation is greatly reduced and their emotional involvement with the outcome is negligible. Even events perceived as important, if they are uncontrollable, tend to provoke behavior known as "learned helplessness"—"No matter what suggestions I make, the boss won't change anything." If sales reps don't think they have a chance of making a difference, they'll give up. If managers don't think they have a chance of making a difference, they'll give up too.

Learned helplessness is an important contributor to the trip to lethargy. It's a great way to generate "I am nobody" feelings. George "will never amount to anything" because he feels he can't make a difference. "We gotta keep him around" because George isn't that important (to us). Learned helplessness is a contagious disease. George is lethargic because he's lost interest in the job; your managers are lethargic because they've lost interest in him.

UNMANAGEABLES

The process of becoming is not easy. Some people have great difficulty achieving authenticity and joyfulness and make little progress toward achieving self-actualization. Although this book is not about paranormal behavior, from time to time you and your managers will experience it, not only in others but occasionally in yourselves.

One source of such paranormal behavior is the counterfeit self, a term used to describe the distortion of the actual self. It helps your managers understand not only why you can't sell everyone but also why you can't manage everyone. Some people distort their actual selves by refusing to accept and process properly their perceptions of themselves and the world around them. If they were to compare their descriptions of themselves with descriptions furnished by other people who knew them well, their self-descriptions would be severely at odds with the consensus. Sometimes this distortion is healthy, as when people confined to wheelchairs choose to overlook their handicaps and go about living normal lives. But some cases of actual-self distortion can lead to grandiosity: the "Napoleons" seen roaming the grounds of mental institutions. Less severe cases—not uncommon among sales reps—manifest exaggerated notions of their skills, intellect, or personal qualities. These people can be difficult to get along with. They live in the tranquil consciousness of their effortless superiority. They don't take suggestions well.

Some people distort their actual selves by accepting only those perceptions that maintain or enhance their feelings about themselves and excluding those perceptions that don't. All people deny their shortcomings to some degree ("That's just the way I am"). Life would be too painful if they didn't. Severe cases, however, involving blocking large portions of oneself and the world from awareness, can lead to extreme withdrawal: the catatonics crouched motionless in the corners of psychiatric wards. People with less severe cases can also be difficult to get along with. Their refusal to engage in any form of self-actualization can lead to behavior that is hard to predict—arrogant at one moment, moody the next.

Some people try to escape from their actual selves by defining themselves through association with other people or groups and adopting other people's attributes, skills, and characteristics as their own. Much of this kind of behavior is normal, such as the positive reactions to teamwork (We did it!) and feelings of belonging (My alma mater). But severe cases of actual-self escape can lead to membership in antisocial groups (fascist parties, for example) that provide "I am nobody" people with "I am somebody" feelings. As with other counterfeit selves, people with even less severe cases can still be difficult to get along with; they appear to live vicariously through others rather than coming to grips with their own lives.

Karen Horney's notion of the "idealized self" adds another dimension to the notion of the counterfeit self. The *idealized* self, as distinguished from the *ideal* self, results from people *substituting* their ideal selves for their actual selves. They begin to identify themselves more with who they want to become than with who they are. This idealized self takes control, not because it is more appealing than the actual self, but because identification with the ideal self solves more of the person's problems. Horney, one of the most prominent psychotherapists of this century, called self-idealization "a comprehensive neurotic solution." A person's drive for self-actualization is "shifted to the aim of actualizing the idealized self." Unfortunately, the idealized self of the neurotic tends to contain a higher fantasy content than the ideal self of the mentally healthy person. Thus, the aim of actualizing the idealized self is never met. Horney identified the neurotic solutions served by self-idealization as expansive, self-effacing, and resignation.

The *expansive* solutions attempt to seek mastery over life as a way of conquering fear and anxiety. Some people become narcissistic, holding "an unquestioned belief in [their] greatness and unique-ness." These people, despite their self-centeredness, may give the impression of caring about others but, being essentially unrelated to other people, are unable to maintain close relationships with them. Some become perfectionists, seeking "the flawless excellence of the whole conduct of life." These people despise others for their inability to measure up to their standards yet cannot admit to errors or mistakes of their own making. Others become vindictive, with "an impelling need for triumph." These people are extremely competitive and treat others as stepping stones in their paths to the top. People attempting expansive solutions try to get even by putting other people down.

The *self-effacing* solutions attempt to seek help, protection, and love as ways of living with feelings of inferiority, guilt, and failure. These people tend to "subordinate [themselves] to others, to be dependent on them, to appease them." They cannot assert them-selves or take chances for fear of offending someone. Always feeling abused, their way of getting even is to try to make other people feel guilty.

Resignation is the third neurotic solution. These people seek their freedom through the absence of conflict: "withdrawing from the inner battlefield and declaring [themselves] uninterested." They tend to live as if they "were sitting in the orchestra and observing a drama acted on the stage, and a drama which most of the time is not too exciting at that." The hallmark of their behavior is the "absence of any serious striving for achievement and the aversion to effort." They resent efforts to influence them. They resist change. They try to get even by passive resistance.

It is unfortunate that the world contains people with counterfeit selves and "I am nobody" feelings. They do not function well. Even more unfortunate, though, is that these people are not always easy to recognize, let alone help. The mechanisms for preserving their sense of self are complex and often beyond the understanding of even the most sophisticated therapist. Your managers can't bring out the best in everyone. No one should expect them to.

Fortunately, the world is full of authentic, joyful people who are actively engaged in becoming the people they want to become. These are the people who exhibit *positive* life stances. The next chapter discusses these people. They represent real opportunities for managing motivation.

NEWTON'S LAWS

XX. You can't polish horse shit.*

Refers to situations, NOT people.

Chapter 25

Opportunities

Authenticity is a pattern of behavior derived from the experience of people who know themselves and respect and like what they see. Authentic people perceive their world and themselves realistically. They are in touch with their values and beliefs, and they are for the most part aware of how their values and beliefs influence their behavior. They use their intellect to question and modify their values and beliefs, to solve their problems, and to monitor and control their feelings. They understand context: when to follow the rules, when to estimate probabilities, when to play hunches. They are realistically proud of themselves. They take responsibility for their behavior.

Realistic self-awareness and the capacity to take full responsibility for their behavior permit authentic people to relate effectively to others, for to experience one's own uniqueness is to delight in the uniqueness of another person. Authentic people are aware of and have respect for the individuality and variety of other people's values and beliefs, of the differences among people in how they go about solving problems, and of the intensity and importance of other people's feelings. Hire authentic people. They make good sales reps. They are likely to become your Eagles.

LIFE STANCE

Life stance is a term I use to describe a person's overall frame of reference—the set of attitudes, assumptions, and expectations people hold about themselves, other people, and the world in general. It comprises, for instance, people's attitudes toward money, assumptions about their health, and expectations for their children's future. The product of the life stance is the overall, general, consistent, and stable way people look at things: whether they tend to be optimistic or pessimistic, cheerful or gloomy, trusting or suspicious, friendly or reserved, brave or timid, and so on.

Life deals people many blows. People with positive life stances learn to distinguish between damage to themselves and damage to their perceptions of themselves. They view damage to themselves as a normal and inevitable consequence of living. It can sometimes be meliorated by the appropriate exercise of caution but is never entirely within their control. Whether they experience damage to their perceptions of themselves, however, is a situation within their control. As Eleanor Roosevelt so eloquently expressed it, "No one can make you feel inferior without your consent." People with a positive life stance tend to be happy, and vice versa. They also tend to be good parents, good spouses, good lovers, good friends, good co-workers, good employees, and tremendous sales reps. Eagles typically have positive life stances. Even people with positive life stances, however, can feel pessimistic, gloomy, suspicious, and helpless from time to time. No one deserves to be judged for his or her performance on a down day.

CHANGE

Denial. Anger. Bargaining. Depression. Acceptance. According to Elizabeth Kübler-Ross in her book *On Death and Dying* (MacMillan, 1969), these feelings and behaviors are the stages people experience as they face the inevitability of death from a terminal illness.

Academics and practitioners interested in studying the process of managing change in organizations have noticed the same feelings and behaviors in people trying to cope with changes of a much lesser magnitude than death.

Change is loss. No matter how beneficial the change is likely to be in the future, a promotion, a transfer, a termination, a territory realignment, a new technology that replaces old work habits, and so on, all require people to give up something; for example, mastery of a now-obsolescent skill, relations with favorite customers or co-workers, or the comfort associated with predictable work activities. A person may eagerly seek and await a promotion. Once the expectation becomes a reality, however, shock sets in, self-doubt surfaces, and the stages of dealing with change begin. Some people work through these stages and arrive at acceptance quickly. (A positive life stance helps.) Others experience difficulty in working through these stages, often getting bogged down in depression.

For example, a sales rep has just been informed that his territory has been realigned. Here's what your managers can expect to hear:

Denial: "You've got to be kidding, Jane! Add up the accounts again. There's got to be a mistake somewhere."

Anger: "God damn it, Jane! I'm losing two of my best accounts—ones I developed from nothing—and you sit there and talk about 'fairness.' Your dumb decision is going to cost me money."

Bargaining: "Wait a minute, what if you let me keep these two accounts and I'll work extra hard to convert some prospects in my new territory?"

Depression: "Aw damn! Well, go ahead. But don't expect much enthusiasm from *me*."

Acceptance: "Hey! These new accounts are working out great. And my travel time is reduced, too!"

Your managers should recognize these stages and help their people work through them. Reflective listening and reality checks are helpful tools at your managers' disposal. (And don't forget, your managers need help, too.)

"Managing change" is a redundancy. Without change you wouldn't need managers. You could just hire a few administrators to do the daily paperwork. But most of your people will resist change. High-performance sales forces, however, try to keep these people to minimum numbers by helping them work through change situations. The Eagles in your organization—and that includes nonsales-rep Eagles, manager Eagles, executive Eagles, and every other employee whose behavior is Eagle-like—expect and welcome change because of the excitement and challenge that accompany it.

DIVERSITY

Like managing change, managing diversity is a redundancy. If it weren't for diversity we wouldn't need managers. Diversity issues have always been around. After all, everyone is different. But nowadays fairness and fiat have accelerated the need to capitalize on the benefits that a diverse workplace brings.

The major obstacle to capitalizing on diversity is bias. We all have biases. The challenge is to recognize them in ourselves and make sure they don't propel us into making bad decisions. Like the resistance to change, most of your people will continue to feed their biases. They need help. Your personal example is a good place to start. The Eagle-like people in your organization will welcome diversity because it enlarges the pool of available Eagles and helps ensure the continuity of your organization by reducing the chance of cultural vitrification.

ADULT LIFE CYCLE

As people age, their goals and the direction of their lives undergo significant changes. The nature and timing of these changes, often referred to as the *adult life cycle,* are predictable and can provide your sales managers with useful insights into people's behavior. Although behavioral scientists differ in their terminology and views about the timing of the stages of the adult life cycle, most agree that people of similar ages experience similar decision points in their lives. These points involve the same issues for nearly everyone and mark transitions from one stage of adult development to the next.

The female reader is cautioned that most of the ideas contained in the notion of the adult life cycle have been drawn from studies of men. Foremost among those who have conducted studies on the adult male are Daniel Levinson and his colleagues at Yale University. Less is known about women in this respect. Nevertheless, the use of the androgynous word "people" assumes that (1) the female reader will recognize what does and does not pertain to her, and (2) regardless of personal relevance, she is interested in improving her understanding of the behavior of the men around her.

Roaring Twenties: Most early decisions people make about the direction of their lives are made for them by parents, teachers, friends, and role models. People's early goals in life are somebody else's goals that they have agreed to adopt. Some people join the family business because Mom and Dad always assumed they would. Whether people drop out of high school or go on to college may depend on the presence or absence of a teacher's encouragement. Some people become mechanics because they were told they were handy with tools. Some people attend college because their coach helped them develop a great jump shot. Some people major in philosophy because they liked their Ethics professor. Some people join a rock group because they want to be like Bruce Springsteen. Perhaps a few people can resist these external pressures and become forest rangers because they love the great outdoors, but these people are in the minority.

Some time around age 20—depending on the amount of one's formal education and experiences such as the armed services—people enter adulthood ready, or not so ready, to make their mark on the world. They are shot from the mouth of a cannon, a cannon aimed for them by other people.

If people have resolved the issues that provoked their teenage rebellions, the twenties become the decade of living up to other people's expectations. The initial job choice is heavily influenced by their education, which in turn was heavily influenced by the advice and expectations of others. The decision to get married (most people do) is more often a function of familial and societal expectations than raging glands. The same applies to having children. Social and lifestyle decisions tend to revolve around establishing relationships at work, in the family, and the new neighborhood. Life is exciting. Everything seems new. People's bodies are in great shape. Life will go on forever. For most people, the twenties are happy times, full of fun and games.

The major problem for managers working with people in their twenties is that despite great reserves of energy and enthusiasm, the young sales reps seem like loose cannons on the deck. They jump from task to task—sometimes from job to job—with little sense of commitment, loyalty, or follow-through. Easily bored with routine, impatient to "get ahead," unfocused in purpose, and oblivious to consequences, they seem "immature." No wonder! They are trying, to use a phrase coined by Tony Athos, my former colleague at the Harvard Business School, "to win the game that others have designed."

Encourage your managers to be patient. The roaring twenties don't last forever. Make sure your managers spend time with the young Eagles. Despite the tendency to fly in circles, they learn fast. Soon they'll be flying high.

Desperate Thirties: Slowly but surely, as the Roaring Twenties draw to a close, the excitement of adulthood turns into pressure, and other people's expectations begin to feel like prison. People as they turn 30 begin to wonder what life is all about. Why am I here? What am I doing? Is this all there is?

Some time around the 30th birthday—give or take a few years—people begin the process of, to use Levinson's phrases, "Settling Down," and a few years later, "Becoming One's Own Man." For most people, this period is traumatic. They must either reaffirm the choices they made in their twenties—job, spouse, family, friends, lifestyle—or they must make changes. Basically the issue is: Do I go on like this, or do I start afresh while I still have the chance? (For some people, this issue is never addressed or resolved, and they continue appearing immature and irresponsible until trauma trips them up.)

These choices are tough ones to think about, let alone make. Do I really want to be a sales rep (engineer, reporter, truck driver, school teacher, or whatever) for the rest of my life? Why did I marry *her*? Did I really want kids? Do I really want to continue living like this?

People typically examine every option and assess the consequences. If their jobs seem to be providing them with sufficient satisfaction and evidence for future self-actualization, if their spouses and families (all fantasies aside) look like a realistic return on their emotional investment, if their lifestyle appears sufficiently satisfying and the prospects for enhancing it seem pretty good, then no changes seem necessary. But any or all of these decisions can be (and often are) made in the negative. It's no wonder then that job and lifestyle changes are frequent around age 30. This period is fantasy time. It seems a good time to start over. People go back to school, leave the drafting board for sales positions, give up teaching for work in a laboratory, decide it's time to get married or divorced. Because a lot of people get married in their early twenties, the "seven-year itch" that shows up in the thirties is probably less a biological phenomenon than a life-cycle one.

Whether earlier decisions are reaffirmed or new decisions substi-
tuted, two important consequences occur. The first is that the decisions people now make are recognized as being owned by them. The
game is no longer someone else's game. It's now their game and it's
to be played by their rules:

> "I'm glad I quit that engineering job. This sales job will give
> me a better chance to make money."

> "I'm glad I went into sales. I think I can really make some-
> thing out of myself."

> "It's time I got married. I need to settle down and take on
> some responsibility."

The second consequence is that people set goals for themselves that
they seek to achieve in light of their decisions regarding job, family
situation, lifestyle, and so on. Making decisions about the future
and determining goals in life are seldom formal procedures. Few
people sit down with pencil and paper and list their strengths and
weaknesses, needs and wants. More often it is the growing realization, stemming from days, months, and even years of staring at
themselves in the mirror while they get dressed in the morning,
that they must take ownership of their goals in life and ownership
of the ways they choose to achieve them. By now they are somewhere in their early thirties and ready to take responsibility for
their lives.

Along with "Settling Down" and "Becoming One's Own Man," many
people begin the relentless and desperate quest for "Success." This
trip is not necessarily joyful, however. Nor is it to be confused with
strivings for authenticity or the process of self-actualization, although all these developmental activities can coexist. The Desperate Thirties are the years to "make it." The quest is relentless
because making it doesn't allow for letting up. It is desperate because failing to meet one's own goals is harder to take than failing
to meet the goals other people have set. (It's only in retrospect that
the thirties seem so desperate. When we start playing the game,

it's fun.) People in their thirties are playing the game they designed. It's called "Winner Take All."

If their definition of success is tied up with their work, their job has now become their career. The focus now is on "getting ahead." They put in longer hours, often at the expense of marriage and family. Social life drifts away from old friends toward peer relationships at work. Lifestyle decisions (for example, house, neighborhood, clothes, cars, vacations) tend to center on outward appearances rather than inward gratifications. Exercise is less for fun and more for "staying in shape." Life takes on a frantic quality.

The major problem you and your managers face in trying to work with people in their thirties is that, despite this newfound purpose and sense of responsibility, people in their thirties seem so consumed by their own careers that they become oblivious of all else, so intent on building a skill base and attracting the attention of their superiors that they tend to lose touch with the interests of other people (including both their families and their subordinates). At best, their egocentricity makes them boring; at worst, it makes them merciless. Yes, they are good at getting short-term results. But their desire for "visibility" can lead to behavior that is upsetting, even threatening, to others. It is easy to leave these people on their own, because they seem to act like perfect "self-starters." But managers should be trying to help people in their thirties maintain a healthy, balanced perspective on their careers and outside activities, while channeling their work-related energy into efforts that contribute to high levels of performance.

Hurricane Years: As the thirties draw to a close, the pressure people have been feeling turns to anxiety. The drive for "success" gives way to feelings of doubt. It's time for another period of self-assessment: How am I doing? Am I getting what I want out of life? Will I "make it"? As Charlie Brown's little sister observed in one of the "Peanuts" episodes, "Life isn't an essay exam. It's a series of multiple choices."

Some time around the fortieth birthday, people enter what for most of them is the most traumatic decade of their lives. Some writers call the forties the "Hurricane Years." It's the period when people start nervously checking the scoreboard that goes with the game they designed. And they must come to terms with death and failure. If they don't do it voluntarily, trauma will sooner or later force the issue.

Until the early forties, mortality is more or less an intellectual issue. As people begin to lose parents, older friends, or colleagues, however, earlier feelings of "It won't happen to me for a while yet" give way to "What if it does?" What was once an intellectual issue fast becomes an emotional realization. People's bodies begin to supply them with additional evidence of aging. Their once firm flesh is beginning to wrinkle. The lenses in their eyeglasses are getting more expensive to replace. People no longer jump over the net after two hard sets of tennis to commiserate with the losers; they settle for shaking hands. Other people start calling them "sir" or "madam," as if these new terms of respect were secret passwords acknowledging their admittance to senior citizenship. Their bodies team up with their minds to force them to consider "Is there enough time left to do what I set out to do?"

People must also come to terms with failure, because the forties provide them with one of the great paradoxes of life: they fail whether they succeed or not. By the time people are in their early forties, the evidence on the scoreboard is becoming clear: they're either going to make it (that vice-presidency, that endowed chair, that seat on the Stock Exchange, that Pulitzer Prize) or they're not. But either way, they lose.

How do they lose if it appears they're going to make it? They lose because they realize that the satisfaction of making it wasn't worth the price they paid. As one of my friends said not long after he was made chief executive officer of a major corporation, "I busted my butt for this?" One of the great tragedies of life is to achieve in maturity the dreams of youth.

If it appears to people that they're not going to make it, they lose because they realize that they couldn't live up to the expectations they had placed on themselves. They seem to have failed in life.

The process of coming to terms with death and failure can take several years to work through, but by their late forties, most people have made some major adjustments. In mentally healthy people, the actual self has become more "real," the ideal self has become refined, and new life goals can be established. The "successful" CEO turns to a life of public service. The army major takes early retirement to teach mathematics in junior high school. The superintendent of the loading dock becomes active in coaching Little League baseball. The "failed in life" feelings were only temporary after all.

In addition to goal substitution, people turn their attention to parts of their lives they had previously short-changed: romantic interest in their spouses is revived; more time is planned in activities designed to get to know the kids (now teenagers); college reunions are anticipated with joy; recreation (for fun again) and entertainment (without clients and customers) become integral parts of the weekly plans. If they are fortunate enough to be working in organizations that care about them and their growth and development, people in their late forties can begin to shed their fear of failure. Work loses its desperate intensity. Opportunities to take chances and be creative become more plentiful.

For some people, however, the period of readjustment is painful. A negative life stance and "I am miserable" feelings can lead to a number of less-than-desirable outcomes, particularly if the death and failure issues are not addressed and resolved or the individuals work in callous organizations that chew people up and spit them out. For these people, the hurricane years can be a dreadful experience. They must somehow escape from the situations they have created for themselves. Even people with positive life stances toy with the idea of escape (the hurricane years ignore no one), but people whose life stances have not equipped them to deal with the issues of death and failure, or who have swept those issues under the carpet, feel that they have no choice but to escape.

One form of escape is "The Big Change." The idea here is "A new job (spouse, lover, or whatever) will reduce my discontent and I can keep doing what I'm doing." Another form of escape involves chemi-

cal dependency. Most people in their forties who toy with the idea
of escape drink too much only temporarily, but those determined to
escape may become alcoholics or otherwise drug addicted. A third
form of escape, more rare, is to play "Runaway." This form includes
everything from the development of a formal mental illness such as
schizophrenia to joining the "zither and bead set" in San Francisco.
And, of course, if people can't escape, their bodies may do it for
them. It's called a heart attack.

In summary, the forties are termed the Hurricane Years for good
reason. It's a time of personal upheaval—sometimes gentle to the
self and invisible to others, sometimes brutal to the self and bizarre
to others. For the manager who cares about people this is the time
to show people in their forties understanding, compassion, and patience. The bizarre behavior will probably pass, and you and your
managers will be rewarded with a rejuvenated employee, one with
added measures of maturity and commitment.

Nifty Fifties: If the issues of the thirties and forties have been
satisfactorily resolved, usually by the time the fiftieth birthday
rolls around, people know who they are. Furthermore, if their life
stances are positive, they like and accept who they are. They have
entered an age of maturity, actively pursuing the new goals and life
direction formulated during their late forties. Now, authenticity is
easier to come by, because they no longer feel a need to appear as
anybody other than who they are. They have collected (and dispensed) enough silver and gold chips to feel, if not joyful, at least
reasonably close to it. Their actual self has become more "real,"
their ideal self more achievable, and they are experiencing the
gradual closing of the gap between actual and ideal self, along with
an awareness that it will never close entirely.

Families of people in their fifties, although probably more sepa-
rated geographically than earlier, are more united emotionally. The
presence or prospect of grandchildren gives people a true sense of
generation, of being a part of humanity. With time to expand their
interests, people learn to take pleasure in everything from Mozart
to jazz, from posters to Picasso, from gardening to tennis. And
speaking of tennis, how about those side-line comments people in

their fifties overhear when their backhand return-of-serve catches their opponents flat-footed: "Terrific shot for someone that age." The pressure's off. The fun is back. They were able to return that serve because nobody would have been surprised if they couldn't. No wonder they're called the Nifty Fifties.

The major impact of the fifties isn't on individuals, however, it goes through them to the people around them. These are the giving years, when people begin in earnest to pay back all they have received from others. No longer keeping things to themselves in order to get ahead, they look for proteges whom they can mentor and for whom they can exercise their power and influence. Helping others get ahead has become their primary work motive (and, not incidentally, helps them become even better sales reps and managers). The fifties are the platform for the wisdom years that lie ahead.

I can't understand why so many sales organizations put up with loose cannons on their decks and ignore or try to terminate people who are so potentially valuable and inspiring as people in their fifties. Unless they have been badly mismanaged in the past and, consequently, exhibit apathy and learned helplessness, people in their fifties have a lot left to give. Your managers should be encouraged to tap this vast resource. A lot of elderly Eagles around are more than willing and able to help younger Eagles learn to fly even higher.

WOMEN

Are women different? The glib answer to this question is "obviously." A more reflective response might be "yes, but. . . ." Women work, marry, form families, build relationships, and fashion lifestyles. They attempt to satisfy their physiological, safety, social, ego, and self-actualization needs. They work to feed and clothe themselves and their families. They strive for recognition, accomplishment, and advancement. The relative need for achievement, affiliation, and power varies as much among women as it does among men. No evidence suggests that women are any less committed than men in their striving for authenticity, in their trip to joyful, or in their desire for self-actualization.

Many female readers, particularly those over forty, would agree that women experience an adult life cycle similar to that experienced by men. The issues may not be identical, particularly for women who do not work outside the home, but the questions are the same: Who am I? What am I doing? What do I want? Is this all there is to life? The fact that the issues may not be identical among men and women is a consequence of biology and society. Because most women can bear children, this fact is an imperative. Men around age thirty are trying to decide the future direction of their lives. So are women at this age, but the ones who are mothers typically include the welfare of their children in this decision to a much greater degree than do the fathers. And the ones who are not yet mothers feel time running out, the pressure to accept or reject the imperative. Most thoughtful people would agree that the thirty-something crisis is even more stressful for the average woman than it is for the average man.

In the forties' midlife crisis, both women and men have to resolve the issues of death and failure, although to the childless woman, failure may include feelings of lost opportunity. The regeneration of the mentally healthy man that typically occurs in the late forties may be delayed in the mentally healthy woman as she attempts to deal with impending menopause and an "empty nest" or intensified feelings of lost opportunity. A woman's Nifty Fifties, therefore, may begin a few years later than a man's.

In the same way that a woman's body places added demands and responsibilities on her, so does society. In many cases, "her upbringin' is her downfallin'." Despite the best efforts of some parents to raise their children to become *persons,* societal forces channel little boys to become men ("Be strong") and little girls to become women ("Be nice"). The consequences can be enormous, because society sets *expectations* based on gender and establishes *conditions* based on gender. For women, the expectations and conditions are seldom in sync.

Societal expectations for men are simple: They are to work and earn the wherewithal to support themselves and their families. The vast majority of men accept these expectations—*not* to work is *not* okay. Furthermore, men are considered successful only if they are able to convert a job (a set of activities for which one gets paid) into a career (a planned, timed sequence of work and work-related experiences that leads one into and through a series of positions to which one aspires). Societal conditions for men are generally supportive of these expectations, and organizations (basically subsets of society) are designed to implement these expectations. Put another way: organizations are established in such a way as to provide men with the opportunity to work and to get ahead.

Societal expectations for women are more complex and still in flux. In the old days, a woman was expected to confine her work to the home and provide only nonfinancial support for her family. A woman worked outside the home only if she "needed" to, that is, to satisfy physiological and safety needs. Before the 1960s, the majority of women accepted these expectations—to work (and thereby take a job away from a man) was *not* okay. Societal expectations began to change in the 1960s, however, and it became not only okay for a woman to hold a job, it was okay for a woman to pursue a career. Because it was still okay in some circles not to work but not okay in others, a woman was faced with a choice—one few women were prepared by upbringing to make.

As the decades passed into the 1990s, however, more women have become comfortable with choosing, which has resulted in a variety of female lifestyles and acceptable societal expectations: women not working outside the home; women holding jobs and perhaps building careers outside the home as "hobbies"; women holding jobs and building careers outside the home as forms of personal fulfillment; and women—single, married, or head of household—working from economic necessity.

Although the variety of lifestyles and okay societal expectations has increased for women, the societal conditions to support these lifestyles and okay expectations have not kept pace. Organizations by and large have been slow to accommodate women's needs and unique roles. Equal opportunity, equal pay, child-care systems, and attitudes and behavior are but a few of the societal conditions in which further progress is necessary and desirable. No wonder that the discrepancies between societal expectations and societal conditions leave many women with a sense of frustration and disillusionment. It's important that your organization accelerate its efforts to accommodate women and that your male managers appreciate that Eagles come in both genders.

NEWTON'S LAWS

XXI. The only constant is change.

Heraclitus

Chapter 26

High Performance

Although sound recruiting and hiring practices are critical if your sales managers are to match sales reps' skills and interests to the realities of their assigned sales tasks, too often the realities of the sales task receive insufficient attention. As a consequence, potentially successful people underperform or, even worse, underperformers walk off with all the prizes.

What does the selling job require? Although selling can be defined as the creation and maintenance of mutually profitable account relationships, the selling job itself focuses on the performance of tasks—a word that comprises the technical, interpersonal (intraunit), and relational (interunit) activities involved in accomplishing sales objectives. Because most work involves a series of tasks, coordinated and sustained over time, the selling job requires people to perform a number of activities, all of which they are presumed to be qualified for, and perhaps even interested in performing.

These activities vary in complexity, time horizon, importance, urgency, stability (the degree to which the requirements are subject to modification), autonomy (the degree to which the tasks require supervision and control), risk (the degree to which failure can be tolerated), tangibility (the degree to which feedback is available), and so on.

The selling job provides people with rewards for the performance of these activities. Some are extrinsic, such as salaries, fringe benefits, and working conditions; others are intrinsic, such as challenge, recognition, and the realization of personal growth.

The selling job also provides people with resources to facilitate the performance of these activities. Some resources are physical, such as sales tools, audiovisual equipment, and company cars; others are in the form of people who help, teach, and encourage.

Ideally, the selling job should also provide clarity: for Me, what I'm supposed to do; for You, what you're supposed to do; for Us, how we are supposed to work together; for The Situation, what the characteristics of the sales task are, how it is to be performed, and what the accompanying protocols are supposed to be; for The Context, what the meaning and purpose of these activities are and how they fit into business-unit strategy; and for The Outcome, what the expectations and standards of performance for these activities are.

The Me usually encompasses, but is not restricted to, skills, aptitudes, interests, attitudes, and needs. Common sense dictates that the skills and aptitudes a person brings to the selling job must be compatible with the requirements of the tasks involved, or the person's satisfaction with and performance on the job will be low. It takes more than wanting to be a sales rep to become a good one.

In a similar way, a person's interests must match the requirements of the workplace. No matter what the degree of skill or aptitude, if a person has little interest in the specifics of what he or she is paid to do, he or she is unlikely to perform well.

The attitudes people bring to the workplace also establish their potential to perform well. People's needs are entwined with their attitudes about work in general, because people bring to a selling job a variety of needs; some they expect work to satisfy, others they don't. Beyond the satisfaction of physiological and safety needs, work can provide people with opportunities to satisfy some of their social, ego, and self-actualization needs; channel their needs for achievement, affiliation, and power in constructive ways; become more authentic and joyful; and collect more gold and silver chips. The greater the degree to which work can be made a major source of their sales reps' need satisfaction, the more opportunity your sales managers will have to motivate them.

Most people need the opportunity to perform well as part of their natural growth and development. But do people perform well because their job is satisfying, or is their job satisfying because they perform well? A great deal of research has been directed toward answering this question, and the evidence is almost overwhelming: Under normal circumstances, high job satisfaction is the consequence of perceived high job performance. That is, the better people see themselves performing on the job, the greater will be their satisfaction with the job. This conclusion is based on a lot of evidence suggesting that intrinsic needs, such as accomplishment and recognition, are more powerful motives than extrinsic needs, such as pay and working conditions. Apparently, most people can put up with peeling paint in their offices and a little less in their paychecks if they are given reassurance that their work is important and their efforts are appreciated.

COMPETENCE

The degree of competence people bring to the workplace obviously establishes their potential to perform well. What is competence and how does it influence the behavior of other people? In the early 1960s, Ted Leavitt, a former teacher and colleague of mine at the Harvard Business School, conducted a series of experiments designed, in part, to answer this question. Groups of executives and students were shown a short movie of a sales rep making a presentation to a customer. The viewers were asked to rate the sales rep's performance along a number of dimensions, including product knowledge, understanding the customer's problems and operations, competence, trustworthiness, and likability. One version of the movie showed the sales rep doing most of the talking and reacting to (rather than questioning) the customer's comments about his problems and operations. The viewers of this version nearly always rated the sales rep "average" on all the dimensions. Another version of the movie—with the same actors and exactly the same product information disseminated by the sales rep—showed the sales rep doing less talking, listening more to the customer, and by asking questions exhibiting more understanding of the customer's problems and operations than in the first version. The viewers nearly always gave this sales rep "excellent" ratings along the same dimensions. What does this experiment show? Is competence perceived by the customer as technical skill or as the seller's ability to understand the customer's situation? Are trust and liking necessary before a sales rep is perceived as competent, or do perceptions of a sales rep's competence produce feelings in the customer of trust and liking? Here are the findings:

☐ The most dramatic shift in the ratings between the "excellent" and "average" sales presentations was in the category of understanding the customer's problems and operations. This category was the "leading indicator" for the ratings on the sales rep's competence.

☐ Even though the data on product information were kept constant in the "excellent" and "average" sales presentations, the "excellent" presentation produced higher product-knowledge ratings.

☐ The shift in ratings between the "excellent" and "average" sales presentations was much greater for competence than it was for trustworthiness or likability. Competence was the "leading indicator" for the sales rep's ratings on trustworthiness and likability.

It seems, therefore, that people's perceptions of other people's competence are more a function of how they perceive the other people's interest in and knowledge of their situation than their evaluation of other people's technical knowledge—so much so that, holding technical knowledge constant, the more a person is perceived to be interested in and knowledgeable about another person's situation, the higher the latter's evaluation of the former's technical knowledge will be. This conclusion makes intuitive sense: the more a sales rep appears to understand the problems and situation of the customer, the more relevant (and complete) will the sales rep's technical knowledge seem to the customer.

Feelings about other people's competence also seem more likely to produce corresponding feelings about their trustworthiness and likability than vice versa. This conclusion is compelling but less intuitive than the previous one. Many people hold that, in order to believe what other people are saying, they first have to trust and like them. These experiments suggest the opposite: The more a person is perceived as competent, the more readily another person comes to trust and like that person.

The lessons here for your sales managers and sales reps seem clear: Sufficient technical competence to get the managing and selling job done is an absolute necessity, but technical competence is not enough. Competence also involves understanding the problems and situations faced by others and applying one's technical skills to solving those problems and improving those situations.

In high-performance sales forces, where motivation is managed well, the competent people (those who perform their jobs well) are successful (earn the tangible and intangible rewards for their performance) and the successful people are competent. In low-performance sales forces, the reverse is true: The incompetent people (those who perform poorly) earn the rewards, and the unsuccessful people end up doing all the work.

SELLING BEHAVIOR

Stage I. The Music Man

The concept of what constitutes competence in selling behavior has changed over the years. Back in the days before World War I (these dates are approximate and vary widely with the sophistication of individual firms), success in personal selling was regarded as a function of a sales rep's personality, his or her ability to charm customers. The mythology prevalent at the time was "good sales-men are born, not made." Consequently, few firms gave sales reps any training or supervision. Little attention was given to perfor-mance evaluation, and straight-commission plans were relied on to weed out the unfit. Many of the general public's notions about sales reps stem from the sales practices of this era, as dramatized by several playwrights. Willy Loman of Arthur Miller's Death of a Salesman is a failure because he can no longer impress his custom-ers; Harold Hill of *The Music Man* is so popular and entertaining that he can persuade anyone to buy almost anything. Today, buyers require more from sales reps than charm.

Stage II. The Animated Catalog

After World War I, increased industrialization and competition caused many prospective buyers to pay closer attention to product performance than they had in the past. In response, sellers began to train their sales forces in communicating product features. The prevalent mythology was that "a good salesman is someone who knows his product." Although this stage was a vast improvement over the reliance on sheer personality, sales presentations tended to become mechanical repetitions of product information that could have easily been transmitted through a good product brochure. The "canned presentation" or "product pitch" produced a generation of sales reps who were little more than animated catalogs. Today, buyers can get this kind of information from their computers.

Stage III. The Magic Formula

During the 1930s, as competition became intense and sales forces grew with influxes of young, inexperienced sales reps, sellers' training activities began to include attention to buyers' needs. Sales reps were trained to make sales presentations designed (1) to manipulate buyers' reactions and (2) to give sales representatives confidence in their ability to sell by providing them with a "road map of the sale"—a series of steps through which they were to lead their customers. A prime example of this approach was AIDA: Attention-Interest-Desire-Action. Success in personal selling was considered a function of how well a sales rep could communicate the benefits, as opposed to the characteristics, of the product line. The tactic was to "sell the sizzle instead of the steak." The prevalent mythology was "a good sales rep controls the sale." Again, this stage was a vast improvement over the animated catalog—it acknowledged the presence of a customer and the legitimacy of his or her needs—but it produced a generation of sales reps who equated selling with outwitting the customer through a "magic formula." Today, buyers easily recognize manipulation when they experience it.

Stage IV. The Problem Solver

During the 1950s, many sales executives realized not only that sophisticated buyers were becoming familiar with all these probing and closing techniques but also that customers' thought processes seldom followed the sales rep's road map. Furthermore, buyers were demanding more professionalism from sales reps, asking them to take more of an advisory role. "Let me make up my own mind" was becoming a common buyer's plea.

In response, sellers' training activities began to stress the sales rep's role as a consultant. The sale became a two-step process: (1) to help the customer determine and articulate the real problem he or she faced and (2) to present the product's benefits as a partial or complete solution to that problem. This kind of selling forced the sales rep to become more analytical than in the past and more sensitive to the wide range of factors affecting a buyer's decision. The sales rep became less manipulative and more responsive. Success in personal selling was considered a function of how well a sales rep could help customers determine the criteria for choosing among alternative products, as well as how skillful the sales rep was in demonstrating how his or her products satisfied those criteria. In this fashion, a good sales rep literally "allowed the customer to buy." By helping customers define their own needs, the sales rep entered the sale at the very beginning and, in this way, could often place his or her products at a considerable competitive advantage.

The sale itself was the final segment in a decision process that the sales rep had helped the customer work through in its entirety. The prevalent mythology now refers to "consultative selling." Customers are more responsive to this new breed of professionals, and sales reps themselves feel prouder about what they do for a living. A new generation of sales reps is growing up as problem-solvers.

Obviously, these four stages did not fully replace one another; they have evolved to complement one another. A measure of personal acceptability, technical competence, and flair for "selling the sizzle" is required to be an effective problem-solver. However, a sales rep who cannot handle this last stage—a role similar to that of a management consultant—will increasingly become beleaguered as customers come to expect this kind of professional activity. Indeed, there may be no alternative to Stage IV. Increases in the efficiency of alternate methods of delivering a sales message—advertising, cable television, telemarketing, videophones, and so on—and a tendency to automate and computerize purchasing decisions may sound the death knell for all but the most sophisticated, professional sales forces. Remember, a lot of purchasing agents are Eagles, too. The competitive environment is prompting many firms to realize that controlling their cost of goods sold requires top-notch people backed up by sophisticated computer systems. It won't be long before only one kind of sales force is left: Eagles who respect and can work effectively with the Eagles on the other side of the desk.

Whereas a magic formula can be readily taught to large groups in a relatively short period of time, Stage IV has one drawback: consultative selling requires a depth of skill and understanding that can only come through one-on-one training by someone highly qualified in this kind of selling. The best approach is to provide your sales reps with field sales managers who view the development of their Eagles into super problem-solvers as their number one priority.

NEWTON'S LAWS

XXII. Feed your eagles; starve your turkeys.

Conclusion

Leadership is the management of motivation. In effective business units managing motivation is an activity performed at all management levels. No element of motivation is overlooked; none is overworked. Managing motivation begins with managing one's own behavior: professional behavior is a given. From that point on, however, the responsibility for activities that constitute the management of motivation differs from one management level to the next. How well does your business unit manage motivation? Here is a checklist:

How well do your *senior executives* (in particular, your chief executive officer)

☐ define and articulate your business unit's mission and values?

☐ formulate effective strategies to accomplish that mission and perpetuate those values?

☐ gain the commitment of your business-unit personnel to pursuing that mission and embodying those values?

☐ set challenging and meaningful business-unit objectives?

☐ determine policies and procedures that gain spontaneous and reasoned support for the business-unit's mission and values, and facilitate the implementation of its strategy?

☐ avoid Magic Bananas?

☐ create the cultural and workplace climate conditions for high performance?

Positive responses to these questions help ensure that business-unit personnel know where they are going, how they are going to get there, and what they can expect to receive from their efforts and commitment. Managing motivation begins at the top. It's the responsibility of your senior executives.

How well do your *middle-level managers*

☐ reinforce the definition and articulation of your business unit's mission and values?

☐ contribute to the strategy-formulation process with facts and ideas?

☐ channel the energy and activities of your business-unit's personnel toward the successful implementation of business-unit strategy?

☐ define the desired behavior of the sales force?

☐ help gain the commitment of your sales force by providing them with the resources to do their jobs well?

☐ implement policies and procedures in ways that improve the workplace climate and stimulate high levels of performance?

☐ take responsibility for the hiring, care, and maintenance of your Eagles?

Positive responses to these questions help ensure that business-unit personnel are given the opportunity, support, and encouragement to fly high, and the latitude and inspiration to fly free. Middle-level managers create conditions for high performance by seeking to achieve congruence between your sales reps' desire to achieve personal growth and development and your business unit's desire to achieve its strategic objectives. Managing motivation continues through the middle levels of management. It's their responsibility, too.

How well do your *field managers*

☐ reinforce the definition and articulation of your business unit's mission and values?

☐ understand how your business unit has chosen to compete in its marketplace?

☐ understand how business-unit policies and procedures influence the behavior of their sales reps?

☐ understand desired sales-force behavior?

☐ recognize how their own behavior encourages conformity between the desired behavior of their sales reps and the actual behavior they observe?

☐ exhibit the kind of professional behavior toward their sales reps that builds trust, provides challenge, and inspires high performance?

☐ care for, listen to, and understand the *behavior* of their sales reps?

☐ recognize and reward competence in their Eagles?

☐ feed your Eagles and teach and encourage them to fly high?

Positive responses to all these questions almost guarantee a high-performance sales force. Creative leadership at all levels of the organization is the key ingredient to managing motivation. As managers gain positions of increasing responsibility, the scope of their leadership activities enlarges from dealing successfully in small, face-to-face, individual and group situations to dealing successfully with larger, more complex groups of people. At the same time, the responsibility inherent in their leadership positions enlarges from accountability for the successful performance of relatively simple tasks to maintaining the continuity of whole organizations.

Index

A

Acceptance, 166-167, 228, 229
Accomplishment, 239, 245
  see Mission, Sales, Task
  recognition, 204-205, 211
Account, 95, 155, 157, 229
  see Expense
  conversion/maintenance, 75
  profitability, 75
  relationships, 243
Accountants, *see* Business-unit
Accounting department, 102
Achievement, 204, 208-211, 239,
  245
ACM, *see* Average
Active listening, 167
Activity/activities, 135, 163-175,
  243
  see Professional, Sales, Training
  performance, 244
Administration, 174-175
Administrative
  activity, 13
  task, 131
Adult life cycle, 231-239
Advancement, 205, 239

Advertising, 25-26, 31-35, 54
  see Consumer
  agency, 26
  allowances, 42
  budgets, 25
  campaigns, 26, 32, 34
    efficiency, 31
    performance, 34
  copy, 26
  effectiveness, conditions, 31-32
  funds, 22
  media, 26
  message, effectiveness, 31
  objectives, 34, 35
  stages, 35
Aesthetic value, 44
Affiliation, 208-211, 240, 245
Agents, 41
AIDA, *see* Attention
Anger, 228, 229
Applicants, 87
Appraisal, *see* Continuing, Performance
Argyris, Chris, 11
Attention-Interest-Desire-Action
  (AIDA), 249
Attitude, 158, 204, 244

see Sales, Work
Attributes, 28
  see Purchaser
  clusters, 29
Authenticity, 167, 223, 227, 238
Authoritarian leaders, 10
Average cumulative monthly stand-
  ing, 109
Awareness, 178
  see Customer, Self-awareness

B

Bagging, 107
Barter/bartering, 228, 229
Behavior, 4, 15, 66, 88, 127, 131,
    143, 145, 157, 172, 174, 180,
    189-192, 204, 206, 212, 227
  see Consumer, Creative, Field,
    Goal-directed, Manager,
    Managerial, Organization,
    Professional, Purchasing, Re-
    sponsible, Sales-force, Sell-
    ing, Trusting, Variety-seek-
    ing, Work-related
  consistency, 145
Bird dogging, 57
BLS, *see* Bureau
Bonus(es), 98-99
  see Group
Brand, 37, 38, 41
  see Competing
  loyalty, 24
  preferences, 40
  reputation, 32, 41
Brown chips, 189, 190, 191
Bureau of Labor Statistics (BLS),
    119, 120
Business
  see Customer
  character, determination, 22
  meetings, 110
  relationships, 105
Business unit, 3, 5, 25, 48, 78
  competitive position, 129
  deliberations, 36
  distinctive competence, 60
  marketing strategy, 47, 92, 131
  mission, 60, 123, 253, 254
  objectives, 35

resources, 101
selling task, 83
values, 253, 254
Business-unit
  accountants, 39
  decisions, 35, 43
  executives, 53
  marketers, 39
  marketing strategy, 61
  news, 106
  objectives, 42
  personnel, 124, 253, 254
  policies/procedures, 255
  strategy, 3, 5, 244
Buyer(s), 28, 249
  see Potential, Prospective
  decision, 250
  motivation analysis, 24
  self-confidence, 30
Buying
  criteria, 28
  decision, 29
  habits, *see* Consumer

C

Call reports, 77-80
Call-report system, 77
Canvassing, 57
Carrot and stick management, 212
Challenges, 12
Change, 18, 228-230, 237
  see Strategic, Task
Channels, 39
  see Distribution
Charisma, 8, 9, 155
Charismatic
  leader, 8
  leadership, 8
  management, 155
Chief executive(s), 13
  officer, function, 12
Chip
  see Brown, Gold, Plastic, Silver
  accumulation, 183
  collecting, 177-182, 184
  deprivation, 183
  dispensing, 184-193
  refusal, 183
  sufficiency, 184

suspicion, 183, 193
Clarity of expectations, 159-160
Clients, 26, 100
Climate, 135-141
  see Style-Climate, Work, Work-
    place
  managers, 125-200
  variables, 137-140, 148
Coaching, 144, 163-164
Cohesiveness, 10
Cold calling, 57
Collecting, see Chip
Command, chain, 11
Commission, 69, 99-100
  plans, 99, 248
Commitment, 59-61, 81, 147, 232
  opportunities, 169
Committed organization, 13
Communication(s), 169
  flow, 80
  objectives, 33
  skills, 9
Company executive, 25
Compensation, 4, 71, 95-104
  see Financial
  plans, 68, 95-97
  systems, see Sales-force
Competence, 14, 159, 245-247, 248,
    255
  see Sales, Technical
Competing brands, 43
Competition, 39, 40, 41, 76, 249
  see Price
Competitive
  activities, 78
  advantage, 250
  environment, 3, 51, 88, 131
  factors, 96
  position, see Business unit
Competitor, 22, 38, 55, 68, 146
  pricing tactics, 42
  product, 34, 44
Complex tests, use, 86
Compliance, 155
Compliments, 178, 184
Conceptualization, ability, 3
Conflict, 139, 187
  see Internal
Congruence, 166, 167, 254

  see Goals
Consensus, 223
  opportunities, 169
Consistency, 150
  see Behavior
Constructive criticism, 191
Consultative selling, 250, 251
Consumer
  acceptance, 43
  advertising, 54
  attitudes, 34, 41
  awareness, 34
  behavior, 34
  buying habits, 24
  decision making, 23
  durables, 55
  loading, 42
  memories, 34
  nondurables, 55
  products, 55
  sophistication, 41
Consumption, see Per-capita
Context(s), 9, 151, 152, 198, 244
Contextual misunderstanding, 154
Continuation training, 91-92, 93
Continuing appraisal, 117-119
Contractors, 147
Controls, 68, 138, 172-174, 222
  see Sales
Corporate performance, 99
Counseling, 164, 170-171
  see Nondirective
Creative
  behavior, 16
  goals, 60
  leadership, 7
Creativity, 83, 132, 136, 144, 173
  see Technical
Criteria, 28-29
  see Buying
Criticism, 145, 189-193
  see Constructive, Pollution-free
Crown prince syndrome, 93
Cumulative sales, 109, 110
Customer, 5, 23, 24, 34, 41, 77, 97,
    246, 249, 250
  see Direct, Indirect, Potential, Pro-
    spective, Second-order
  awareness, 34, 97

businesses, 73
complaints, 37
dissatisfaction, 74
familiarity, 83
functional risk, perception, 31
group, 24, 26, 73
influentials, 47
inquiries, 37
perception, 24
personnel, 146
relationships, 76
risk perception, 31
satisfaction, 25, 36, 97
self-image, 32, 33
service, 41
sophistication, 38
specialists, 74
surveys, 131
symbolic risk, perception, 31
vendor preferences, 26

D

Dealer(s), 36, 38, 49, 53
  discounts, 42
  inventory, 37
  margins, 54
  sales representatives, 42
Decision(s), 13, 29-30, 39, 128, 234, 235
  see Business-unit, Buyer, Buying, Deployment, Distribution, Pricing, Product-policy, Purchase, Selection, Short-term, Strategic, System, Tactical, Training
  maker, 158
  making, 13, 15, 59, 144-145
  see Consumer
  processes, 28
Decision-making
  activities, 66
  processes, 25
Declining stages, 35, 45
Defensible niche, 25
Delegation, 144
Delivery selling, 55
Demands, see Environmental, External, Internal
Demographic(s), 18

analysis, 24
Demonstration, 163
Denial, 228, 229
Dependability, 83
Dependence, 158
Deployment, 74-75
  data, 78
  decisions, 75
  issues, 74
Depression, 228, 229
Desperate Thirties, 233-235
Development, opportunities, 206
Differentiation, see Product
Direct
  customers, 56
  distribution, 37
  selling, 60
Direction, unity, 11
Discount, see Dealer
Discounting, 156
Disincentives, 105
Dismissal, 118-119
Dissatisfiers, 205
Dissonance, 30
  see Postpurchase
Distortion, 165, 166, 223
Distribution, 34, 35-39, 54
  see Direct, Exclusive, Intensive, Physical, Selective
  channels, 35, 41, 53
  selection, 36
  decisions, 26, 37, 39
  networks, 22
  policies, selection, 36
Distributors, 41
District managers, 110
Diversity, 230
Door-to-door selling, 97
Dyadic relationships, 149
Dynamic salesmanship, 9

E

80-20 rule, 92-93
Eagles, 78, 83, 84, 91-93, 96, 102, 109, 120, 123, 124, 130, 155, 164, 170, 175, 184, 200, 201-255
Early warning, 118
Earning opportunities, 74

Economic growth, 22
Education, 232
  loans, 103
EEOC, 114
Empathy, 166
Employment contract, 117
Encouragement, 188-189
Engineers, 101
Entrepreneurial
  selling, 57, 97
  spirit, 99, 100
Environmental
  demands, 14
  forces, 128
  opportunities, 18, 23
Evaluation criteria, 114
Excellence, 136
Exclusive distribution, 37
Execution, 11, 13
Executive(s), 24, 45, 120, 127, 130,
    190
  see Business-unit, Company, Mar-
    keting, Sales, Sales-force,
    Senior
  levels, 33
  skills, 3
Expansive solutions, 224, 225
Expectations, 240
  see Clarity, Performance, Societal
Expense accounts, 102
External demands, 14

F

Face-to-face situations, 11, 16
Field
  managers, 51, 58, 93, 118
  sales managers, 5, 87, 92, 114,
      130, 132, 140, 148, 163, 164,
      170, 172, 175, 251
    behavior, 140
    role, 127-129
  supervision, 127-134
    barriers, 129-132
    lack, 129
  training, 91, 92
    activities, 129
Final warning, 118
Financial
  analysts, 101

compensation, 95
  problems, 164
Finessing, 156-157
Fixit
  management, 132-134
  managers, 164
Flexibility, 145
Foundation, 1-61
  see Leadership, Strategy
  overview, 3-6
Freedom, 144
Fringe benefits, 102-104
Frustration, 181
Function, see Chief, Leadership
Functional
  characteristics/needs, see Product
  improvements, 40, 44
  information, 24
  risk, see Customer
  value, see Product

G

Generics, 37
Goal(s), 26, 177
  see Creative, Management-devel-
      opment, Performance, Self-
      fulfillment, Work-related
  congruence, 98
  determination, 13-14
Goal-directed behavior, 206
Gold chips, 178, 180-186, 188, 218,
      238
  deprivation, 183
Goods, 59
Government, 22
Grievance procedures, 66
Gross rating points, 48
Group(s), 16, 209
  see Customer, Sales, Social
  activity, 11
  bonuses, 99
  dynamics, 136
  identity, 139-140
  interaction, 138
  life insurance, 103
  loyalty, 151
  situations, 11, 16, 255
Growth, 9, 136, 199, 213, 245

see Economic, High-growth, Human, Managerial
opportunities, 206, 219
stage, 35, 44
Guilt, 173

H

Handyman syndrome, 132
Herzberg, Frederick, 204-206, 218
Hierarchy of Needs theory, 206-208
High involvement, 27
High performance, 6, 7, 129, 133, 153, 216, 243-251, 253, 254
atmosphere, 148
organization, 14
sales organizations, 66
sales-force, 3, 16, 18, 20
High-gross margins, 32
High-growth
market, 147
situations, 121
High-performance
organizations, 54, 68, 101, 129
sales, 87
sales executives, 71, 89
sales forces, 48, 68, 77, 78, 80, 83, 87, 91, 92, 120, 123, 124, 154, 230, 247
executives, 84
sales organizations, 46, 67, 119, 127
Hiring guidelines, 85-86
Historical quotas, 80
Historical sales, 80
performance, 80
Hospitalization, 103
Human
growth/development, 205
resources, 11, 213
Hurricane Years, 235-238
Hybrid sales forces, 57-58

I

Incentives, 105-112
Indirect customers, 56
Individual efforts, 13
Individual/organization relationship, 11
Industrial

marketer, 33
marketing, 23
products, 33
Industry
familiarity, 83
norms, 96
Inferiority/insecurity, 181
Information, 155
see Functional, Postpurchase
Initial training, 91
Initiative, 83, 144
Innovation, 11, 13, 18
Inspiring, 170
Institution(s), distinctiveness, 15
Institutional
commitment, gain, 14-15
integrity, defense, 15
mission, definition, 14
mores, 135
Insurance, *see* Group, Major
Integrity, 159
Intensive distribution, 38
Interests, 150
Internal
conflict, 66
order, 15
demands, 14
Interpersonal
differences, 12
relationships, 156
Introductory stage, 35
Inventory, 37
see Dealer
Invisible supervisor, 123-124
Involvement, *see* High, Personal

J

Job, *see* Selling
Job dissatisfaction, 205
Job performance, 245
Job satisfaction, 136, 204, 205, 221
Jobbers, 41

L

Labor
see Skilled
supply/demand, 96
Leader(s), 8-16

see Authoritarian, Charismatic, Price
responsibility, 12
Leadership, 7-16, 59, 123, 124, 253, 255
see Charismatic, Creative, Multiple
foundation, 1-61
functions, 12-16
relationships, 10-11
responsibilities, 14
revisionists, 11-12
role, 6
situations, 9-10
traits, 7-9
Learned helplessness, 222-223, 239
Leisure time, 22
Life
cycle, *see* Adult
stance, 228
Listening, 164-169
see Active, Reflective, Responsive
Loans, *see* Education, Second-mortgage
Losses, 40
Low-performance
organizations, 128
sales force, 54, 247
sales organization, 67
Loyalty, 232
see Brand, Group, Vendor

M

Magic bananas, 67, 71-72, 74, 253
Major medical insurance, 103
Management
see Carrot, Charismatic, Fixit, Motivation, Sales-force, Sales-management, Scientific
by objectives (MBO), 81
philosophy, 79
policies/practices, 69, 79
system, 67-69, 123, 124, 127, 128
team, 79, 110
Management-development
goals, 85
programs, 48
Manager(s), 10, 52, 69, 84, 85, 95, 116, 165, 125-200, 203-206,

208, 217, 221, 229, 230, 232, 239
see Climate, District, Field, Fixit, Middle-level, Product, Sales, Style
behavior, 158
Managerial
behavior, 129, 143
content, 131
growth, 195-200
talent, 132
Manipulation, 171-172
Manpower needs, 79
Manufacturing, 3
ease, 26
Margin, 80, 95
see Dealer, High-gross
Marginal profits, 40
Market, 37
see High-growth
coverage, 70
segment, 25, 26
segmentation, 23-25
share, 41
Marketer, 25, 33
see Business-unit, Industrial
Marketing
see Industrial, Push
activities, 42, 97
approaches, 25
efforts, 23, 28, 44
executive, 5, 21, 48, 49, 55
intelligence, 78
objectives, 34
plans, 91
development, 21
strategy, 3, 4, 6, 21-46, 47, 48, 55, 58, 60, 61, 70, 130
see Business unit
formulation, 21
tactics, 55
Marketplace, 44, 96, 100, 255
Maslow, Abraham, 206-208
Mass production, 46
Masserman, Jules, 12
Maternity loans, 103
Mature stages, 35, 41
McClelland, David, 208-210
McGregor, Douglas, 211-213

Middle-level manager, 254
MBO, *see* Management
Mind reading, 157-158
Minimal prerequisites, check, 86
Mission, 127
  see Business unit
  accomplishment, 17
  clarity, 19
Missionary selling, 56, 57, 96
Misunderstanding, 153-154, 165
  see Contextual, Situational
Monopoly, 25
Morale, 10
Motivation, 177-193, 247
  see Buyer
  management, 3, 5, 7, 16, 20, 50,
    55, 59, 105, 123, 124, 128,
    131, 134, 136, 155, 216, 253-
    255
Motivational
  activities, 60
  factors, 205
Motivation-Hygiene theory, 204-206
Motivators, 133, 205, 207, 208,
  217, 219
Motive, 28
Multiple leadership, 9
Mythology, 69-70, 71, 248, 250
  see Sales-management

N

Needs, 206-208, 211, 218, 239, 241,
  245
  see Hierarchy
Networks, *see* Distribution
Newsletters, 105-106, 109
Niche, *see* Defensible
Nifty Fifties, 238-239, 240
Nobody/somebody, 180-182
Nondirective counseling, 166

O

Objective
  data, 24
  standards, 115
Objective(s), 242
  see Advertising, Business, Busi-
    ness-unit, Management,
    Marketing, Quantitative,

Sales-force, Short-term,
  Time-period
overgeneralization, 15
selection, 21
Obsolescence, 18
One-on-one
  relationships, 149
  training, 251
On-the-job training, 91
On-the-spot praise, 187
Openness, 159
Operating decisions, 66
Opportunism, 15
Opportunity/opportunities, 18, 22,
  30, 106, 113, 116, 148, 173,
  181, 182, 192, 213, 221, 227-
  242, 254
  see Commitment, Consensus, De-
    velopment, Environmental,
    Growth, Product, Responsi-
    bility
  deprivation, 19
Organization(s), 3, 8, 9, 11, 19, 59,
  65, 73-82, 84, 111, 151, 216,
  230
  see Committed, High-perform-
    ance, Individual/organiza-
    tion, Low-performance, Reor-
    ganization, Sales, Sales-force
  behavior, 212
  character, 13
  charts, 66
  contintuity, 16, 50, 52
  demands, 11
  effectiveness, 50
  options, 19
  perpetuation, 12
  purpose, 17
  resources, 12, 19
  structure, 67
  task, 9
  values, 155
  viability, 10
  vitrification, 88
Organizational
  approach, 70 commitment, 10
  efforts, 13
  layers, 3
  policies, 127

skills, 9
structure, 13
Outcome(s), 152, 153, 160, 198,
  222, 237, 244
  see Win-win

P

Packaged goods, 33
Paid vacations, 103
Paradigms, 173
Paternity loans, 103
Penetration, 40
  pricing, 40
Penetration-pricing strategy, 60
People, 201-255
Per-capita consumption, 45
Performance, 16, 69, 84, 96, 113,
  136, 155, 159, 221, 244
  see Activities, Advertising, Corpo-
    rate, High, Job, Sales, Sales-
    force, Style-performance,
    Task
  appraisal, 113-121, 130
  comparison, 76, 77
  criteria, 114
  evaluation, 248
  expectations, 244
  goals, 118
  standards, 123, 138, 185, 244
Performance-appraisal
  periods, 96
  systems, 113-115
Personal
  attributes, 114
  characteristics, see Purchaser
  development, 203
  distance, 145
  growth, 133, 203, 244, 254
  involvement, 26
  protocol, 135
  qualities, check, 86
  risk, 199
  selling, 6, 53, 97
  style, 150
  traits, 114
Personal-selling activities, 55
Physical distribution, 36
Planned activities, 18
Plastic chips, 185-186, 188

PM, see Push
Point of purchase, 33
Point-of-sale, 32
  promotional efforts, 53
Policy/policies, 4, 6, 65-72, 137,
  203, 253
  see Distribution, Management, Or-
    ganizational, Pricing, Prod-
    uct, Promotion, Public
  combination, 70
  manual, 65
  system, 63-124
Pollution-free criticism, 190-193
Position, 155
Positioning, 48
  see Product
Postpurchase
  dissonance, 30
  information, 30
Potential, 76-77
  buyers, 25
  customer, 26, 31
Power, 154-155, 208-211, 239, 245
  internal balance, 15
Practices, 69, 70
Praise, 145, 153, 163, 187-189
  see On-the-spot, Public
Predictability, 145, 150
Premium
  see Price
  prices, 39
Price(s)
  see Premium
  competition, 41
  leader, 41
  premium, 41
  range, 39
Pricing, 34, 39-43, 54
  see Penetration
  decisions, 26
  latitude, 39, 41
  maneuvers, see Tactical
  policy, 39
  tactics, see Competitor
Proactive strategic decisions, 18
Probation, 115-116, 171
Problems, 221-226
  see Sales
Procedures, 4, 6, 65-72, 137, 253

system, 63-124
Product
see Competitor, Consumer
  attributes, 27
  auxillary services, augmentation, 45
  benefits, 97, 249
  characteristics, 27, 38
  class, 24
  differentiation, 33, 38, 40, 41
  durability, assessment, 23
  familiarity, 83
  features, 40
  functional
    characteristics, evaluation, 23
    needs, fulfillment, 24
    value, 43
  life cycle, 39, 43, 45
  line, 33, 49, 73, 91, 249
  see Product-line
  managers, 78, 101
  novelty, 39
  offerings, 54
  opportunities, 22
  placement, 27
  plans, 192
  policy, 34, 43-46, 54
  positioning, 25-26
  primary demand, 32
  qualities, 32
  risk, 30
  saturation, 76
  specifications, evaluation, 28
  superiority, 25
  symbolic
    characteristics, evaluation, 23
    differences, 45
    needs, fulfillment, 24
  technical specifications, 33
  variations, 45
Production
  see Mass
  efforts, 44
Productivity, 133
Product-line specialists, 74
Product-policy decision, 44
Professional
  activity, 250
  behavior, 198-200, 255

Profits, 15
  see Marginal
Profitability, 41
Promotability, 84-85
Promotion(s), 36, 42, 179, 205, 206
  budgets, 25
  policy, 103-104
Promotional
  activities, 25
  efforts, see Point-of-sale
  offer, 34
Prospect(s), 28, 29
Prospective
  buyer, 28, 29, 33
  customers, 53
Psychiatric diagnostic devices, 86
Psychographic segments/segmentation, 24
Psychological
  development, 177
  testing, 88-89
Public
  policy, 117
  praise, 187, 188
Pull, 54
  tactics, 33, 54
Purchase
  see Postpurchase
  decisions, 26
  risk, 30
Purchaser, 101
  attributes, 27
  personal characteristics, 27
Purchasing
  agent, 23, 33
  behavior, 26-30
Push, 53
  marketing, 53
  money (PM), 42
  tactics, 33, 53

Q
Quality/qualities, see Personal, Sales, Work
Quality-control problems, 44
Quantitative
  analyses, 76
  data, 48
  objectives, 51

Quantity, *see* Sales, Work
Quotas, 80-82
  see Historical

R

Reactive strategic decisions, 18
Reality, 217-219
Recognition, 106-108, 153, 185,
    187, 206, 207, 218, 239, 244,
    245
  see Accomplishment
Reflective listening, 167-169
Refresher training, 91-92
Regulations, *see* Rules and regula-
    tions
Reinforcement, 187
Rejection, 165, 166
Relationship(s), 149-161, 192
  see Account, Dyadic, Interper-
    sonal, Leadership, One-on-
    one, Reporting
  approach, 11
  theories, 10, 11
Relying, 158
Reorganization, 74
Reporting relationships, 48, 65
Required skills, check, 86
Research and development (R&D),
    60
  breakthroughs, 26
Reseller, 37
Resignation, 225
Resources, 22, 155
  development, 14
Responsibility, 138, 147, 173, 198,
    205, 212, 234, 235, 255
  see Shared
  opportunity, 12
Responsive listening, 167
Responsiveness, 199
Retail selling, 55
Retailers, 41
Retailing, 156
Return-on-investment calculations,
    114
Revisionists, *see* Leadership
Rewards, 138-139, 147
Risk(s), 22, 25, 138, 146, 147, 160,
    173, 209

  see Customer, Functional, Per-
    sonal, Product, Purchase,
    Symbolic
  perception, 30
Risking, 159
Roaring Twenties, 231-233
Rogers, Carl, 166, 167
Role
  see Field, Leadership
  confusion, 153
  models, 13, 153
Rorschach test, 86
Rules and regulations, 65, 66
Runaway, 238

S

Salary/salaries, 22, 100-102, 217
  increase, 205
Sales, 3, 18, 34
  see Cumulative, High-perform-
    ance, Historical, Short-term,
    Trade-sales
  accomplishments, 106
  activity/activities, 28, 47
    quality/quantity, 133-134
  aids, 26
  aptitude, 83
  consummation, 30
  contests, 106-108, 147
  conventions, 110-111
  executives, 4, 5, 8, 12, 26, 48-50,
    54, 55, 58, 69, 71, 75, 105,
    113
  see High-performance
  force, 5, 25, 33-35, 49, 73, 119,
    120, 248-250
  see High-performance, Hybrid,
    Low-performance
  problem, analysis, 6
  groups, 73
  interference factors, 30
  managers, 8, 12, 74, 87, 115, 153,
    172, 174, 189, 195, 200, 204,
    208, 218, 221, 239, 247
  see Field
  meetings, 111-112
  organization, 68, 77, 113, 124,
    130, 154, 170, 221, 239

see High-performance, Low-per-
        formance
performance, 77
   see Historical
positions, 85
presenations, 246, 248, 249
representatives, 4, 26, 28, 29, 33,
        47, 50-52, 55, 58, 68-70, 76-
        81, 84, 85, 88, 92, 93, 95-97,
        100-102, 105-112, 117, 118,
        120, 124, 130-132, 146, 147,
        152, 155, 157, 159, 164, 166,
        188, 190, 191, 193, 203, 223,
        228, 229, 239, 245-251, 254,
        255
   see Dealer, Technical-sales
attitude, 204
competence, 246
control, 163, 173
personality, 248
skills, 243
talent, 170
standings, multiple criteria, 107,
        108-110
tactics, 91
tasks, 55, 147, 148, 210, 244
territories, 49, 75, 76
volume, 33, 34, 75, 97, 98
Sales-call pattens, 33
Sales-force
   see High
activities, 48, 49
behavior, 4, 5, 6, 47-52, 69-71,
        130, 255
compensation systems, 100
efforts, 44
executives, 92
management, 3
objectives, 50-52
organization, 73
performance, 70, 97
strategy, 123
tasks, 50
turnover, 85
Sales-management
   information system, 79
   myths, 69
   system, 69
Salesmanship, *see* Dynamic

Sales-volume gains, 114
Satisfaction, 236
   see Customer, Job
Satisfiers, 205
Scientific management, 10, 11
Second-mortgage loans, 103
Second-order customers, 56
Segments, *see* Market, Target
Segmentation, 48
   see Market, Psychographic
conditions, 24-25
Selection, 4, 83-89
criteria, 83
decisions, 71, 85
methods, 85-87
procedures, 68
Selective distribution, 38
Self-actualization, 11-12, 208, 211,
        213-217, 218, 223, 224, 239,
        245
Self-awareness, 227
Self-confidence, 161, 173, 178, 207,
        211, 217
   see Buyer
Self-deception, 180, 181
Self-deprecation, 180, 181
Self-development, 218
Self-effacing solutions, 224, 225
Self-esteem, 177, 184, 203, 213, 218
Self-fulfillment, 212
goals, 212
Self-image, *see* Customer
Self-loathing, 180, 181
Self-respect, 179
Self-worth, 211
Selling
   see Consultative, Delivery, Direct,
        Door-to-door, En-
        trepreneurial, Personal, Mis-
        sionary, Retail, Technical,
        Trade
ability, 86
behavior, 47, 248-251
stages, 248-251
cost, 97
effort, 96
job, 243, 244
requirement, 243
situation, 163

task, 69, 70, 85-86, 93
  see Business unit
Senior executives, 54, 66, 253
Sequential activities, 18
Service(s), 35, 36, 59
  see Customer
  contract, 107, 108
  placement, 27
Shared responsibility, 192
Sharing, 159, 203
Short-term
  decisions, 22
  objectives, 51
  sales, 98
Sidewalk critiques, 163
Silver chips, 178, 180-184, 186-
        189, 218, 238
  deprivation, 183
Situation, 152, 173, 180, 198, 222,
        244, 247
  see Face-to-face, Group, High-
        growth, Leadership, Selling,
        Social
  factors, 151
Situational misunderstanding, 154
Skill(s), 150, 224, 244
  see Required, Sales
Skilled labor, 22
Skimming, 39
Social
  motives, 209
  reference groups, selection, 23
  situations, 180
  units, 136
Societal expectations, 241, 242
Solutions, see Expansive, Self-effac-
        ing
Somebody, see Nobody/somebody
Specifications, 29
Staff specialists, involvement, 86-87
Stakeholders, 12
Standards, 138, 144, 147, 192
  see Objective, Performance
Startup stage, 9
Strategic
  activities, 53
  changes, 69, 74
  decisions, 17-20, 53, 68
    see Proactive, Reactive

planning, 21-23
  support, 70
Strategy
  see Business-unit, Marketing
  foundation, 1-61
Structure, 137-138, 147
Style, 143-148
  see Personal
  managers, 125-200
Style-climate relationship, 146-148
Style-performance relationship, 148
Substitution, 165
Supervision, 123, 248
  see Field
Supervisor, see Invisible
Supervisory
  activities, 129
  tasks, 130
Support, 139, 170, 254
  mechanisms, 144
Suspicion, 155-157, 160, 173
  see Chip
Symbolic
  characteristics/needs, see Product
  risk, see Customer
  values, 41
System, 63-124
  see Call-report, Compensation,
        Performance-appraisal, Poli-
        cies, Procedures, Sales-force,
        Sales-management
  changes, 67
  decisions, 68, 70-71
  modifications, 68

T

Tactic(s), see Pull, Push
Tactical
  decisions, 18, 53-58, 66
  pricing maneuvers, 42
Tactical-pricing equivalents, 42
Target segments, 25
Task
  accomplishment, 11
  change, 74, 75
  definition, 11
  performance, 148
  specialization, 11
Teamwork, 81

Technical
  competence, 247, 250
  creativity, 9
  knowledge, 247
  selling, 56-57
Technical-sales representatives,
    56, 57
Technology/technologies, 22
Termination, 116-118
Territory/territories, 76
  see Sales
  assignments, 70, 74
  design, 79
Thematic Apperception Test, 86
Theory/theories, 203-219
  see Hierarchy, Motivation-Hygiene
  X, 211-213, 216
  Y, 211-213, 216
Time-period volume objectives, 96
Track records, 84
Trade
  cooperation, 36
  selling, 55-56, 57, 96
  territories, 53
  unloading, 42
Tradeoffs, 28, 29
Trade-sales force, 55, 56
Training, 4, 70, 73, 91-93, 123,
    163, 170, 248
  see Continuation, Field, Initial,
    One-on-one, On-the-job, Re-
    fresher
  activity, 87, 91, 249
  decisions, 71
  procedures, 68
  programs, 26
Traits, see Leadership
Tribal continuity, 9
Trust, 155, 158-161
Trusting behavior, 160-161
Turnover, 96, 102, 119-121
  see Sales-force
  reduction, 50, 164

U
Unmanageables, 223-226
Utopianism, 15

V
Value(s), 14, 124, 150, 151, 156,
    177, 203, 227
  see Aesthetic, Business unit,
    Functional, Organization,
    Product
  judgments, 166, 177, 191, 214
Variety-seeking behavior, 27
Vendor(s), 23, 33
  activity, 53
  loyalty, 24
  preferences, see Customer
Volume, see Sales, Sales-volume,
    Time-period

W
Warmth, 139
Warning(s), 118
  see Early, Final, Written
Weber, Max, 8
Wholesaler, 41
Win-win outcome, 171
Women, 239-242
Work, 211
  attitudes, 203, 205
  climates, 137
  experiences, 218
  quality/quantity, 133
Workload, 74, 75
Workplace, 133, 135, 136, 139, 244
  climate, 140, 143, 200, 253
Work-related
  behavior, 198
  goals, 219
Written warning, 118